In a Desert Land

In a Desert Land

PHOTOGRAPHS OF ISRAEL, EGYPT, AND JORDAN

NEIL FOLBERG

ABBEVILLE PRESS PUBLISHERS
NEW YORK LONDON PARIS

For Anna, with love

Front cover: *Sandstorm, Bikat Baraka*
Back cover: *Canyon of the Siq, Jordan*
Page 1: *Sheep grazing on Mount Scopus, Jerusalem*
Pages 2–3: *Moonrise over the Gulf of Eilat, Wadi Hweit, Sinai*
Pages 4–5: *Bird tracks in sand, Sinai*

Editor: Meredith Wolf Schizer
Designer: Laura Lindgren
Production Manager: Lou Bilka

Second edition

10 9 8 7 6 5 4 3 2 1

Neil Folberg can be contacted directly at
folberg@netvision.net.il

Library of Congress Cataloging-in-Publication Data
Folberg, Neil.
    In a desert land : photographs of Israel, Egypt, and
Jordan / Neil Folberg. — [Rev. ed.]
        p.   cm.
    Includes index.
    ISBN 0-7892-0125-9
    1. Israel—Pictorial works. 2. Egypt—Pictorial
works. 3. Jordan—Pictorial works. 4. Palestine in art.
I. Title.
DS108.5.F63 1998
779'.99569—dc21   96-29936

Contents

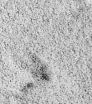

Note to the Second Edition

The original text of this book reflects the events taking place about twenty years ago when I was first photographing in Sinai. Then, an agreement between Israel and Egypt was taking form that led to a full peace treaty. Since that time, there have been numerous other political upheavals whose full effects cannot yet be determined. Some events have been decidedly positive, such as the peace treaty with Jordan in 1995, and others lead me to see much cause for worry. But this was not originally a political book, and I have no wish to make it so now. Then, I had a vision of the land itself, without regard to politics or borders, and that remains. That is what gives these photographs the power and timeless quality that make this second edition possible. We have retained the original text here since it describes the thoughts and experiences that accompanied me during this work— they are as relevant to the photographs now as they were then.

It has only been eleven years since the first edition, but it's nice to know that people still want to see these photographs. Occasionally I get phone calls from strangers in faraway places who have tracked me down and simply must have a copy of this book, even by airmail from Israel. Thanks to all of you! This second edition came about in order to share the beauty of Sinai with more of you, since the economics of publishing and the cost of paper made it impossible to reprint this book in its original larger format. I am reminded of an encounter between Ansel

Adams and Imogen Cunningham at a printing press in San Francisco. When Ansel walked in to find Imogen standing there, he asked her what she was doing there. She replied, "Why Ansel, I'm printing a book. What are you doing here?" "I'm printing a book, too," he answered. Ansel asked her what kind of book she was printing, and in response she held up her hands to form a letter-sized rectangle, saying, "My book is this big." Ansel stretched out his arms and said, "My book is *this big*," to which Imogen replied, "Yes, Ansel, but I like a book that someone can get into bed with comfortably." "Imogen, *two* people can get into bed with my book!" "But Ansel," she said, "what two people would get into bed and then look at *your* book?" So, if before I had a book that two people wouldn't get into bed with, I hope that now I have made a book worthy of someone's bed. For my part, the selection of photographs is more carefully edited—more along the lines of what I had in mind originally. Given advances in printing, I hope the quality and color will be more faithful to my original conception, too.

For nearly three years, while I traveled the world photographing synagogues for my most recent book, Sinai and I have had to get along without one another. Sinai hasn't missed me at all. But if a chill wind blows as I stand out on our porch looking at the nocturnal sky, I think of Sinai. There, mountains have eroded imperceptibly, hotels have been built, and roads paved. Some of the development has been done tastefully, or at least simply, and much else has been done with no environmental concern or planning whatsoever. Some areas have been designated as national parks; I haven't visited them. The wind still blows unimpeded in the vast interior stretches where relatively few go — these places are more or less the same and are likely to remain as they have always been. These are the only places that I have wanted to visit on my infrequent trips to Sinai since *In a Desert Land* was first published. I should be able to tell you what has changed in Sinai, but I can't, since I seek only the unchanging wilderness when I go there. I seek it now, and I plan to go there soon — these words will be true whenever you read them, for as long as I live. This is escapism, I realize, but we in Israel are quite powerless to affect environmental policies in Egypt. And there is no place to which I would rather escape.

In Israel, there is a certain new environmental awareness, but environmental concerns are strictly secondary. As far as I am concerned, few if any wilderness areas remain, though we have many attractive small nature reserves and national parks where people crowd in during certain seasons and leave their trash faster than it can be picked up. The same people litter the ever-expanding road system. Outside the nature reserves, most of the development suffers from poor planning. The Judean Desert and the Negev are heavily utilized by the army for training grounds, as there is nowhere else for them to go. It seems that all we can do is try to minimize the damage, by nature a losing battle. I no longer have a Jeep — there is no place to take it — but it seems like everyone else now has four-wheel-drive utility vehicles and dune buggies. I shudder to think of the sand dunes and desert landscapes that are being torn up by their tires. The beauty remains, but it is nearly impossible to enjoy it in solitude, as I would prefer. This is a fact in this small country.

As I look through the pages of this book, I renew the sensations I felt then. When this work was complete, I thought that no other photographs and no other place could ever provide such satisfaction. I have since made photographs that are equally satisfying to me, but no place on earth can compete with Sinai.

Jerusalem, Israel, April 2, 1996

Introduction

The heart of this book is in Sinai. I have traveled and photographed sporadically in the land of the Nile; in greater depth I've explored the wilderness and hills of Judea as they rise from the Dead Sea of the Jordan Rift toward Jerusalem. For the sake of geographic and visual continuity, I open the book with Egypt, passing through the desert landscapes finally to arrive at the ancient walled city that nestles in the hills at the edge of the Judean Desert — Jerusalem. This I am fortunate to call home, though I would call it that no matter where I lived.

I began photographing Sinai in 1979. The land was addictive in its power to draw me. Only there could I experience the power of wilderness, of open spaces and desert mountains. Had I not been kicked out of Sinai by political circumstance, I would have continued working there, never thinking of anyplace else. With access to Sinai restricted, after Israel ceded the territory back to Egypt, I drew back to get a wider perspective. Sinai was, after all, in the heart of the Middle East, a bridge between continents, between the land of Egypt and the land of Israel. So the time had come to begin exploring and photographing in both of these directions as well.

The challenge of landscape photography is to reduce a limitless expanse to the confines of a two-dimensional rectangle without creating a feeling of confinement within borders. It is necessary to give enough information about the environment so that the imagination can extrapolate beyond the edges of the photograph, to envision what might be beyond the next ridge, to create in the image before the viewer's eyes a mood evocative enough to make him want to wander in his mind through that image. This is the challenge of all landscape work, but Sinai is particularly difficult, for its true beauty is not immediately evident. The beauty of the desert lies less in its small delights — a wildflower, a pool of water — than in the delight of finding these things in the midst of dryness. Then there is the naked, treeless expanse itself, impressive precisely because of its vastness.

So my first task was simply to be there, to look around, to get the feel of the place. This I was able to do through the kindness of Dr. Aryeh Shimron of the Israel Geological Survey. At that time, in 1979, he was making regular trips to Sinai, expeditions that usually consisted of two Jeeps, often with room in one of them for a guest. Needless to say, there were many eager to join these trips, but Aryeh felt that Sinai was something to be shared not only with geologists. Accordingly, he made room for me, a photographer.

We visited mostly the less obviously scenic areas in Sinai, areas of dark-red metamorphic rock and broad, nearly featureless wadis that sometimes go on for great distances. My recollections of these earliest trips are sparse, and most of the photographs I made were trivial. Even when there was something attractive in them, they nevertheless failed to evoke the feeling of the place. Each time I returned from Sinai and looked at my work, I knew there was something missing.

By fortunate coincidence, I happened to read at about that time *On Moral Fiction*, a book by John Gardner. He wrote, "The lost artist is not hard to spot. Either he puts all his money on texture—stunning effects, fraudulent and adventitious novelty, rant—or he puts all his money on some easily achieved or faked structure, some melodramatic opposition of bad and good which can by nature handle only trite ideas. One sort of artist can see only particular trees, the other only the vague blackish-green of the forest. The artist who gives all his energy to texture . . . can say virtually nothing because his work consists wholly of nonessentials."

Reading this confirmed my intuition that the photographs I was making, though occasionally intriguing, missed the mark. First of all, I needed to identify the essence of Sinai and work to capture it while avoiding any reliance on a visual formula to create a superficial unity among the photographs. When you set an ambitious goal, you risk failure. If you fail to set a worthy goal, you risk achieving only something small. I decided to climb a large mountain and set my sights on some distant goal. There was always the risk of falling or choosing the wrong path, but the unattractive alternative was to wander aimlessly though the desert, leaving all to chance, making photographs with no purpose.

The yardstick against which I measured my success was experience. If my photography evoked something of the feeling of the place and created a sense of its proportion—usually vastness—while giving enough information about the landscape to make it seem real, and if, beyond this, the photograph was satisfying as a purely aesthetic object, then I had made a good photograph of Sinai. If not, not. Nothing less would do.

So it was that I found myself, more and more, climbing mountains to get a higher vantage point. The trick was to find a point high enough to impart a sense of the environment without losing intimacy, the feeling of having my feet firmly planted on the ground. This didn't always require height, of course, but more a sense of scale, or *balance*. That's what John Gardner called it, "a proper balance of detail and generality, the particular and the universal." This is a fine line to tread.

I had always to be aware of another danger, the pitfall of color, the merely picturesque, color without content. Indeed, I'd begun this project like all my preceding ones, in black and white. On my first trip with Aryeh Shimron, I brought both black and white and color materials. I processed only a few of the black and white images and threw the rest away without developing them. The reason was simple: the desert consists largely of monochromatic earth colors. These colors are subtle and beautiful, but they translate into black and white as various shades of middle gray. Filters and development controls would have helped create some contrast and interest, but these wouldn't have proved sufficient. I learned such techniques from the master, Ansel Adams, but I also learned from Ansel what it means to "pre-visualize," to decide in advance what statement you're making, how to see the subject, and how to create the final print in accordance with your vision. I didn't want shades of gray, middle or otherwise; I wanted color. I wanted everyone to see the loveliness of the delicate coloration and the way it changed so dramatically according to the season and the hour of the day.

The same map will lead different people to different places. Odd that some find this fact so hard to accept. I am told that a museum curator visited an exhibition of mine and said, "If Francis Frith photographed that area in black and white, why does Neil Folberg need color?" One of the main reasons that Frith photographed in black and white was that color photography had yet to be invented. In their quest for more "scientific" accuracy Frith and many others of his period would almost surely have used and loved color.

Many of us recall the days when "art films" were made exclusively in black and white, and only the slick commercial films in color. In the art world there is a certain snobbishness about black and white. This doesn't concern me; each medium has its uses. Nevertheless, there *is* a danger of mistaking color for content. It is an error I've certainly tried to avoid.

There are those who say that the viewpoint of my photographs is distant. Quite right; but I hope it never seems detached, for my involvement with the subject is intimate. My viewpoint enables you to wander through the photograph as I have wandered through the landscape. You must be given the opportunity to choose your path as I have chosen mine. While walking through the desert, one thinks of many things. I present a setting and a mood (this generally having been determined by my mood when the photograph was made). I want you to use your imagination, to think your thoughts—in short, to wander and wonder. I don't care to confine you by imposing my convictions on you. Derive pleasure from being with me in the places I have been. As John Fowles wrote, "We . . . know that a genuinely created world must be independent of its creator; a planned world (a world that fully reveals its planning) is a dead world."

Egypt

This night was no different from countless others spent in a sleeping bag looking up at the stars glittering in blackness—the same stars I had become accustomed to in the Sinai winters, though in a somewhat different configuration. On moonlit nights (but this night was moonless) the urge to walk through the broad, shimmering wadis of Sinai usually overcame the fear of walking alone at night in the desert. *Wadi* is an Arabic word for the bed of a dried-up river. Or, rather, wadis exist as rivers, but for no more than a few hours a day and only after massive rains. At these times the water pours through the wadi in a torrent, uprooting trees, a deluge of mud and rocks that carries away all in its path. Such rainfall is rare: during the many winters I spent in Sinai, I never saw a flooded wadi. But on a moonlit night, the smooth, even polished *afik* (Hebrew for the part of the wadi where the water actually flows) reflects the moonlight, suggesting the gentle flow of water over the rocky surface.

In the glow of the moon, these rugged landscapes seem softer and less forbidding than in the full glare of the blinding sun. The full moon lights the way like a torch, allowing you to see just enough, just what you want to see. So you go on, picking your way slowly through the rocks and brush, occasionally glancing up at the sky. Vast as this wilderness is, the sky is much larger. For this you keep walking: a promise of something grander.

These walks and the dreams that accompany them are for moonlit Sinai nights, in which there is always a vista of greater vastness over the next mountain, around the bend. Those are views I would have sought forever had the Egyptian–Israeli peace treaty not intruded by returning to Egypt this land of endless vistas. When Egypt became the doorway to Sinai, I decided to enter through Cairo.

During most visits to Egypt, I felt as if enclosed in a glass bubble, a tourist protected from the smells and dirt by a decent hotel and money, but, even more, by a cultural gap that,

however it excited my curiosity, seemed beyond bridging. And yet so much was familiar here. The Nile, broad and quiet, was reminiscent of a childhood near the Mississippi. The pyramids and ancient temples, like so many other locations throughout the world, had become familiar from countless books and photographs.

On certain days, the Egyptian experience was inviting, like settling into a warm bath. But more often it felt like hovering over a whirlpool of chaos and poverty that threatened to suck in the unwary. Nevertheless, these warm and friendly people made me feel a welcome guest. It was undoubtedly this polarity of feelings—the freedom of wandering alone through the vast stretches of Sinai versus the crowded strangeness of life by the Nile, the ancient memories of slavery and liberation, enmity and peace—that contributed to the turbulence felt each time I descended into Egypt. The activity of photography allowed me the pleasure of moving close while maintaining distance at the same time—to record experience without being consumed by it. Being in the land of the Nile required a delicate balance I had never needed before, not in Sinai and not in Judea or Jerusalem.

But now I was lying still in my sleeping bag under the almost Saharan configuration of stars and planets, far from the exotic Arab culture of the lush Nile Valley. Here, in an Egyptian army camp on the far edge of the Western Desert, lying in the dark of a moonless night, I felt as if Egypt had swallowed me whole.

How did I come to be here?

Well, I hired a taxi in Cairo to take me through the Western Desert—but that's the simple answer. My first trip to Egypt was little more than an attempt to gain access to an area in the Sinai that was closed to visitors entering by way of the Taba border crossing near Eilat on the northern tip of the Gulf of Eilat (or the Gulf of Aqaba, depending on your political affiliation in this hotly contested corner of the world). It seemed that the only possible path to freedom in

the Sinai was to reverse the direction the Israelites would have followed had they left Egypt directly for the Promised Land: Jerusalem, Gaza, Rafah, Suez Canal (a swamp in biblical days), Cairo. But that, of course, was not the way they went. Geometrically, the shortest distance between two points may be a straight line, but in the Middle East the most direct path isn't necessarily the wisest. Since I had already adapted myself to some of the intricacies of life here, it seemed shorter to take the long road to Sinai. Nevertheless, what my ancestors navigated in forty years took me ten hours by bus and cost a mere twenty dollars.

My friend Shaked, who had once been director of the Israeli Field Study Center at Santa Katerina in Sinai, was waiting for me in Cairo and had made travel arrangements before my arrival. Shaked, who

had in the past guided me through Sinai in every sense of the word, was now leading tour groups from Israel through Egypt. He would conduct me on a private tour through Cairo and Luxor before we departed together for Sinai. All good friends should be guides, but few are as good as Shaked.

My dusty bus eventually arrived at the outskirts of Cairo, which seemed like a conglomeration of small crowded villages. Even in the center of the city, the buildings are generally low and covered with peeling paint and plaster. Moving through debris that lies over the city like desert sand are millions of people and vehicles—both ignoring all traffic regulations. Riders defy gravity in their ability to leap onto moving buses so full as to make a sardine claustrophobic. The colors, the movement, the noise, the sheer life force contained within the city, effected a hypnotic spell. I was dazzled.

The bus stopped in what seemed to be the middle of the street, and the driver said to me, "This is where you get off." More than a little anxious, I descended three stairs into the maelstrom. Any worries I may have had concerning finding a taxi were efficiently dispelled by the mob that rushed toward me shouting, "Taxi!" I had fleeting visions of being dismembered and carried away in separate cabs, but one of the drivers simply picked up my luggage and walked to his taxi. This had the desired effect, for I followed and the others stepped aside. I was in Cairo, and I had a terrible headache.

My goals in Egypt were limited to seeing and perhaps photographing a bit of the landscape before moving on to Sinai. I was not prepared to undertake the kind of project I had embarked on in Yugoslav Macedonia during 1971, when I had learned the language and lived with the people. Egypt nevertheless demanded a certain flexibility that wasn't necessary in Sinai, where people were scarce. In a small Egyptian village I was likely to become an attraction—especially to the children—no less interesting than a Bedouin with a camel wandering about St. Louis. Shaked and I were often invited into homes to drink tea and chat (Shaked, at least, was fluent in Arabic), and I often felt I was expected to reciprocate such hospitality with a photo.

After a night's rest, Shaked and I drove thirty kilometers south to the Necropolis of Saqqara. The most impressive feature of the landscape is easily seen on a map: Egypt is a narrow strip of irrigated land surrounded by a vast desert. Within this strip is a paradise of luxuriant growth, described in Genesis as being "like the garden of the LORD"—a garden of straitened confines determined entirely by proximity to the Nile. Interestingly, all older photographs made by DuCamp, Frith, Bonfils, and others during the second half of the nineteenth century show the antiquities as if engulfed by desert, far from water

and life. Yet, here they are, the pyramids of Giza and Saqqara, just a few meters beyond the green oasis of the Nile. This was the first photograph I made in Egypt: the Step Pyramid of Saqqara, on the very edge of the Western Desert, just above and beyond the valley of the Nile (page 11).

What people of Cairo and Jerusalem share, along with most other people in the Middle East, is life on the edge of the desert. Here it is green and cool, there the sun blazes and gives no shelter. My friends in Jerusalem often seem surprised when I remind them that a vast desert lies just the other side of the Mount of Olives. They are lulled into a feeling of security by the forests and orange groves one sees during the descent from the hills of Jerusalem to the Mediterranean coast. The desert near Jerusalem, after all, is hidden from the city by the hills. In Egypt, desert cliffs of the Moqattem Hills hang over Cairo, and the desert is visible from most any point in the Nile Valley. Though he may rarely enter it, the desert is ever present in the mind of an Egyptian. So when I came to photograph the pyramids of Giza, I chose the wider view, climbing a bit into the Western Desert (page 23). Desert tombs dwarf the life of the city just beyond.

That evening we left by overnight train for Luxor and spent the rest of the week visiting antiquities and villages in that area. During one of our evenings in Luxor, riding toward Karnak in a horse-drawn carriage, we heard music that to my ear was instantly recognized as "Turkish"—not really Turkish, but the music that the Moslems and Gypsies of Macedonia play and that *they* call Turkish. Drawn to the source, we were invited to stay for a celebration in honor of the Prophet Muhammed's birthday. A little band was playing, and a few men danced in a circle of spectators.

As in Yugoslavia, a spectator from time to time would pass money to the musicians, who would play in his honor. When they finished, his name was called out and he, his family, and friends were blessed with Allah's blessings. I passed some money to them, and when they were done playing, the announcer approached Shaked and asked where we were from. Somewhat nervously, Shaked replied that we came from Israel; we waited to see if we hadn't overstayed our welcome. The announcement came: "May Allah bless our guests from Israel, their friends and families and all of Israel with peace, forever!" Perhaps Israel hadn't surrendered Sinai in vain.

Anwar Helal, a tour operator who handled many of the groups from Israel and had worked with Shaked many times, tried without success to arrange a Jeep for us in Sinai. A Jeep he couldn't get, but a twenty-five-seat bus with driver, mileage, and gas included could be had for the week for three hundred Egyptian pounds. Why not?

When I stepped out of the hotel early Sunday morning, Ali, the bus driver, was spit-polishing the shiny finish of his prized vehicle. You needed sunglasses to look at it. This bus was destined to go the way of all gleaming new objects in the desert, but Ali was determined to delay disintegration as long as possible. He obviously had no idea where we were headed, and I hadn't the heart to tell him.

We were five of us altogether, Ali, Anwar, Shaked, his girlfriend Michal, and myself. We loaded our things into the bus and instructed Ali to set sail for Suez. Whatever Ali had been told regarding the trip, it hadn't included the information that we'd be traveling on desert roads and sleeping outside. So we thought it best to let Ali in on the secret by stages, trusting to his good nature that he wouldn't refuse. Near Suez, we told him to take the tunnel under the Canal. We emerged from the tunnel into the bright sands of Sinai. Though it looked no different than the other side, it felt better. This was my turf, regardless of who holds the title. The role of tourist passed now to our two Egyptian guests.

We turned south. As we drove toward the oil fields of Abu-Rodeis, we passed Ain Musa, the Springs of Moses. Tradition has it that this is the spot described in Exodus 15:27, the place of twelve springs and seventy date palms where the Israelites

rested. This area was so close to the canal and the oil fields that I made no attempt to photograph, fearing the attention of the authorities.

We came finally to a dirt road, a little rocky, but not bad, leading off to the east. Here Shaked instructed Ali to turn. We waited for his reaction. He turned. With a sigh of relief, I wondered how I could have thought he might refuse. He had already shown all the necessary qualifications of daring and boldness in the face of uncertain risks and even danger—and all this within a few blocks of our hotel in Cairo. We had underestimated Ali; he must have been bored on these long stretches of road, unencumbered with traffic.

We arrived finally at a small Bedouin village near Bir-El-Kaseib in an area of deep red sandstone, quite unlike most other sandstone areas I knew in Sinai. This red sandstone had been one of the reasons for the trip. Just as it was getting dark, I set out to climb a hill above the village. The houses and people got smaller and farther away as I climbed higher; at last they were insignificant against the background. I hadn't gone very far, but in this place even a village doesn't count for much. Now I was alone on my windy hilltop, looking at the deep blue darkening sky and the rising moon. It was a very modest viewpoint by Sinai standards, nothing special, but exquisitely beautiful at that moment. Rushing out of the bus, I hadn't taken my camera. But there was no photograph here: the almost full moon in an empty sky hovering over a low, dark landscape with no outstanding features. Anna, my wife and toughest critic, would have eliminated this transparency on the light table. Not every experience is a photograph.

We slept in the Bedouin huts. The next morning, Anwar, Shaked, and I set out on foot for the ruins of the Egyptian temple of the goddess Hathor at Serrabit El-Khaddim. This temple to the protectress of Sinai, the goddess of turquoise, had been built by workers from far-away Egypt come to mine that gem. It was a lonely spot atop a hill facing the Et-Tih plateau,

which divides northern Sinai from southern Sinai. I made a photograph of record, commemorating my achievement in having arrived there with all my heavy equipment on my back. But the light was rather flat and uninteresting.

One gets the impression that the few Egyptians (as opposed to Bedouin) who live in Sinai—and *very* few live here of their own volition—do not much like hiking in the desert. Why should they? In Egypt the desert is overwhelming, always threatening to engulf the slender ribbon of life along the Nile. It is the enemy. Israelis tend to regard it as a place of excitement and beauty, a challenge—though not all appreciate it in the same measure as I. Egyptians seem to dislike it, if not fear it. Anwar was being open-minded by coming with us. He had seen how the Israeli tourists he led through Egypt loved Sinai, and he

was curious to know why. But, then, Anwar was in every way exceptional; he had been to Israel several times (there is no tourism from Egypt to Israel, only the reverse) and even spoke Hebrew well; he had accompanied Minister of Defense Ezer Weizman during his visits in Egypt. I suspect that at one time he must have been part of the Egyptian intelligence service, but his interest and warmth were genuine. So he hiked with us to Serrabit El-Khaddim. I'm not certain that he enjoyed it, but he was trying to see the world through our eyes, and I liked him for it. I would have liked to see his world through his eyes, but the opportunity didn't—and hasn't—presented itself. As I write this, the Egyptian army is suppressing a rebellion by the nation's security forces, and Cairo is under curfew. How much longer will we have to get to know each other?

From Serrabit El-Khaddim we went south a little way toward the manganese mines at Umm-Bugma. During the years that Israel controlled Sinai, it hadn't been profitable to work the mines, so the road fell into such disrepair that even a Jeep could barely negotiate it. We'd heard that Egypt was attempting to mine here once again, so we hoped that the road had been repaired. We came to the point where the road leaves the wadi and begins to climb steeply up the side of the mountain in a series of switchbacks. From where we stood, the road looked unnerving, but Ali enjoyed his adventure. With a shout, he took off, stopping only when we'd reached the top. Here was a truly magnificent view of the red sandstone, with Jebel Et-Tih commanding the entire horizon to the north, a view well worth the trip from Cairo. I was prepared to sit there and wait for two days, if necessary, for the proper light. We made camp in some abandoned buildings, and I hiked off with my equipment to find the viewpoint for my photograph. The sun was down, but there was still a lot of light in the sky, with a touch of red where the sun had been. These colors are subtly reflected in Jebel Et-Tih. In the foreground, acacia trees dot the red wadis around the little village of Bir-Rekiss. There is a sense of place in this slice of landscape.

We spent some time in Wadi Feiran, one of the major oases in southern Sinai, but the Egyptians had paved the road with asphalt, a black snake in the landscape that destroyed the views. All through Wadi Feiran, which is an administrative center, we were followed by a Bedouin who, obviously, had been told to keep an eye on us. Other Bedouin, with whom Shaked had been very friendly in days gone by, avoided us—though one old friend invited us to sleep in his orchard. The road signs in Sinai are those Israel left, but the Hebrew has been covered with black paint. We were likewise unwelcome reminders of the past, but we couldn't be sprayed out with black paint.

On another trip, in December 1984, Shaked and I decided that we had to see what filled that vast empty space on the map to the left of the Nile Valley. The Kimmerly and Frey map of Egypt I had didn't bother to show all of the Western Desert until the Libyan border. This was intriguing: if there wasn't anything on the map, there was surely a lot to see. The only question was whether we'd be allowed to see it. I placed a call to Cairo and told Anwar what we wanted, charging him with finding out whether permits would be needed to visit the Western Desert, getting the permits if necessary, and arranging transport. Loaded with sleeping bags, food, tent, jerrycans, camera, and uncertainty, we flew from Israel. We trusted Anwar to do what could be done, but in Egypt, one never knows.

He met us at the airport and took us to his office, where we organized our things. He had called to find out if we needed permits and had been told that we couldn't get them. He called another office and was told we didn't need them. He gave us each a T-shirt ("Safaga Travel, Travel with us is adventure") and sent us off in our taxi with these parting words: "See you at the police station!"

That was indeed our next stop. We drove southwest from Cairo through Giza, passing the Great Pyramids as we entered the desert. The road was good, but there was really nothing here—no sand dunes, no interesting terrain, no people. We drove for hours through the enormous expanse, virtually all of it flat. We drove through the evening and into the night, arriving finally at a police checkpoint. An officer examined our passports and vehicle registration papers; then he invited us to stay the night and join him for dinner. Shaked explained that we were Jewish and that I observed the dietary laws. In response, the policeman brought me some water and an electric hot plate he'd fashioned out of a heater. We all shared the food I'd brought from Israel. Later, when his own meal had been brought to him from a nearby police station, we realized that this was what he'd offered to share with us. We slept at the little police outpost; Anwar didn't turn up.

By the time we awoke, our policeman had been relieved by another and was free to go home. He lived in Bawiti in the Bahariya Oasis, some forty or fifty kilometers from where we had slept. Dressed in his civilian clothes, he came with us. I made one photograph of the sunrise over the Western Desert. In Bawiti, he took us to the police station to register, and, these formalities concluded, we went to his adobe home to drink sweet tea.

From Bawiti, it is 180 kilometers to the next oasis, a lovely little place called Farafra, whose only village is Qasr Farafra. We were detained on the way for a couple of hours at an army checkpoint. The soldiers bade us sit, gave us tea, and ignored us for what they thought to be a period sufficient to impress upon us their importance and our isolation. Five minutes would have been long enough. We were conducted into the presence of an officer, who politely asked us questions in English. He threw out a quick one in Arabic to Shaked, who pretended not to understand. His tone grew sharper and less polite as he continued questioning us. Then someone else came up behind Shaked, who was smoking a cigarette, and asked him in Arabic for a light. Even I understood that, but neither of us responded. By now convinced that we didn't understand Arabic, they lost interest in us. Israeli spies, they must have felt, would have known Arabic. Another officer entered and said to the first, "They're from Israel, not Libya. Let them go!" Out here, far from Israel, Libya was the closer danger. Not long before, Kaddafi had threatened to drop an atom bomb on the Aswan Dam.

Qasr Farafra is a lovely little village atop a small rise, with neatly laid out streets. The adobe homes are completely enclosed, hidden behind mud-brick walls that line the streets. This was a place I wanted to photograph, but a viewpoint from a little outside the village was necessary. The army had let us go, but had sent with us a soldier who was going to Asyut in the Nile Valley. He wasn't going to let me look around

outside the village and for the rest of the trip made sure I was never more than a few meters from the paved road. So I set off in the direction of the mosque, intending to climb the minaret, but we were sidetracked by the village schoolteacher, who wanted to show us the local art museum. There really was an art museum, filled with scenes of local life that he had painted. There was a natural history museum, for which he had prepared the exhibits. Then there was an ethnographic museum—another of his creations. The three museums were housed in a three-room adobe. The exhibits were nicely done; clearly, he'd put a lot of effort into them. How many visitors could he have had? Though I wanted to see all he had to show us, the sun was getting lower all the time. Shaked had to be in Luxor soon in order to return to Israel, so we couldn't stay the night in Farafra. What could I do? Now he wanted us to see the school, so I resigned myself to an afternoon of sightseeing in Qasr Farafra.

Our soldier, who had left us temporarily, returned and wanted us to follow him. Ready for anything, we were led to the home of the "mayor." His was a very large adobe house, with a veranda opening on a small courtyard in the back. Beyond this was a lovely walled garden with fruit trees and date palms. Very dark, cool, it must have been delightful in the summer. Seated at a table in the garden was an old man with sunglasses, who served us plates of fruit and tea. He gave me a lemon, but I wasn't sure what to do with it. "Eat it," he said. I did; it was very sweet and a little sour, quite unlike any lemon I'd had before. Shaked had already photographed our host seated at the table, but I indicated that I wished to make a portrait of him on his veranda. This wasn't just a picture, but, compared to Shaked's snapshot, a production more befitting his dignity. When my view camera had been secured on its tripod, I posed him on the veranda, where he was joined by one of his grandchildren (page 29). The photograph surprised me; it was a portrait of a place as well as a person. One day, I hope to return.

We drove another two hundred kilometers in the dark, looping back to the east toward Dakhla Oasis. We were stopped at an army checkpoint somewhere near Jebel Edmonstone. This seemed a good place to sleep, so we made camp on the edge of the army base. We lay down under the stars as the lights on the base were extinguished. Looking up at the starry sky recalled desert nights in Sinai and Judea. Feeling so familiar a sensation in a place as strange and distant as this crystallized the conflicting emotions I had struggled with since I had begun my work in Egypt. At one and the same time, I felt more at home and more lonely.

Dakhla Oasis is a lovely place, rolling sand dunes set against the background of limestone cliffs. There are also patches of lush green fields, and, incredibly, a fine mist hung over the cliffs. The sun, risen, had just begun to burn away the mist when we reached this scene. Working quickly, I managed to make some fine photographs in the area (pages 30–31). Then we drove until we arrived at Mut, a little town on the other side of the oasis. Sensing an interesting view, I sought a way to get up a little. There was a hill in the center of Mut, densely covered with adobe dwellings and narrow passageways. Taking my camera, we climbed through the maze, the state of the dwellings becoming more dilapidated the higher we went. We crawled through a hole in the wall of a crumbled house and found we'd

reached the top. Looking over the cabah of Mut, we could see in the distance a sliver of green and the dunes of the desert beyond. I made the photographs that afternoon.

We slept that night at a government-operated rest house in the Kharga Oasis. Our driver disappeared rather mysteriously in the evening; we later found out that the authorities had pulled him in for questioning. We were a bit concerned about having gotten him in trouble, but our fears proved groundless. We passed through the Western Desert without difficulty, having scratched the surface of a potentially magnificent area. I'll probably never know exactly what I missed. An ant's view of his environment couldn't be much different from what we'd seen of the Western Desert.

Our soldier left us in Asyut. Shaked returned from Luxor to Israel. I celebrated the Sabbath in a luxury hotel on the Nile near Luxor. For a religious Jew, the Sabbath is a weekly celebration of rest, Torah study, and family and is therefore most satisfying observed at home, particularly when your home is Jerusalem. Nevertheless, it was a lovely, peaceful Sabbath spent in the hotel garden and on the balcony of my room, watching the waters of the Nile drift by. The day was long, lazy, and hypnotic. The hills to the west of the Nile came to life in the afternoon light, glowing for a while, then fading into darkness as feluccas floated silently by.

PAGE 11: *Step Pyramid, Saqqara.* The earliest tombs consisted of simple mastabas—steps. It is thought that, as construction techniques progressed, the pyramid evolved as a structure with mastabas piled one on top of the other. Since there is little rainfall and virtually no source of water save the Nile here, this greenery extends little farther than the line reached by the waters of the Nile during its annual flood. Hence the Patriarch Jacob's blessing to Pharaoh that the floodwaters of the Nile should reach to his very feet.

PAGES 12–13: *Sacred Lake near the Temple of Amun, Karnak, Luxor, dusk.*

PAGE 14: *Felucca, Nile at Luxor.* This felucca was sailing slowly upriver; when it became clear that it would pass on the other side of the little island, I decided to wait and make the photograph when it reached the point when only its sail was visible. The hills on the west bank of the Nile glow in the afternoon light.

PAGE 16: *Al-Nasser Mosque, Cairo.* This mosque is located in the Citadel of Cairo, next to the more famous Muhammed Ali Mosque, the minaret of which is a landmark visible from most of Cairo. Modest by comparison, this mosque is by far the lovelier of the two. The stone arches recall the impressive interior of the mosque at Cordoba, where this motif is repeated on a much grander scale in the entrance hall.

PAGE 19: *Forecourt, Mosque of Ibn-Tulon, Cairo.* This mosque is inspiring in its perfect proportions and simplicity. I had some difficulty photographing the main court, but I was permitted to photograph its unique forecourt, surrounded by crenellated walls. The play of light and shadow emphasized the perfect spatial relationships and harmony contained within these walls; rising above them is the more mundane architecture of modern Cairo.

PAGE 23: *Pyramids, Giza.* Giza is just outside Cairo, right on the edge of the desert. This photograph shows all the pyramids together, with Cairo and its haze as a backdrop. As vast and sprawling as the city is, it seems dwarfed by the great pyramids.

PAGE 24: *Mawhub, Western Desert.* The most unusual feature of the Western Desert is surely these oases resting in limestone depressions filled with sand. I have never before seen a mist like this hovering over the desert, but this is an unusually well-watered oasis. Clouds tend to gather over water and greenery, while sandy, barren areas reflect the heat of the sun, which dissipates moisture in the sky above.

PAGE 25: *First light, Lake Nasser at Abu-Simbel.* In Maxime du Camp's 1850 photograph of the temple of Abu-Simbel, the structure is more than half buried in sand where it stood by the banks of the Nile. Before the Aswan Dam project was completed, the temples in this site were moved to higher ground well above the water level. Here they stand now, complete with a hollow, artificial hill behind them to simulate the original setting.

PAGE 26: *Street scene, village of Qurna.* Brightly painted houses stand out in an otherwise monochromatic landscape. These adobe homes are cool and comfortable, with spacious rooms.

PAGE 27: *Village of Qurna.* The village is located almost in the midst of the necropolis of Thebes, across the Nile from Luxor. The ancient artisans who built the monuments and tombs must have lived in this area; indeed, one of the tombs belonged to one of those artisans, a man named Sennuden. The current residents of the area also paint—but on the outer walls of their homes, usually to depict the *haji*, or pilgrimage to Mecca. If they have flown to Mecca, they show airplanes. If they have traveled by camel, they depict camels, as in the house in the foreground.

PAGE 28: *Blue door, Bawiti, Bahariya Oasis, Western Desert.*

PAGE 29: *Farafra, Western Desert.* To my great regret, I was not permitted to make a general view of this village, located on a small hill in the Farafra Oasis. The soldier who accompanied us brought us to the home of this local notable, photographed on the veranda of his home.

PAGES 30–31: *Dunes near Dakhla Oasis, Western Desert.* On the map of Egypt, the Western Desert, between the Nile Valley and the Libyan border, appears as a featureless, unpopulated vacuum. I hired a taxi in Cairo to take me through it on the paved road that loops among four major oases. I made this photograph early one morning where these rolling sand dunes meet the limestone plateau in the distance.

PAGE 32: *Dovecotes, village of Sedfa.* Although elaborately decorated, these dovecotes were used only to collect pigeon droppings.

PAGE 33: *Crocodile charm, Island of Sehel, near Aswan.* Francis Frith photographed a crocodile resting by the riverbank near Philae in the 1860s. These creatures are no longer to be found here. Once worshiped as gods, some of them are now spending their afterlife as good luck charms.

PAGES 34–35: *Nubian Village, Island of Sehel, near Aswan.* As I arrived on this island about half an hour south of Aswan by felucca, an old man met me and offered himself as a guide. We first went to his home, where I was served tea while his family watched a 1930s American comedy on television. We then walked through the village, well known for its adobe homes with their barrel roofs. I made this photograph from the top of a hill, where I could get a general view of the village.

PAGES 36–37: *Feluccas, first cataract of the Nile, Aswan.* Before I left Israel, Shaked had suggested that I climb this hill called Kubbet El-Hawa on the west side of the Nile, opposite Aswan. The gently rippling water and the slow-moving feluccas made a late-afternoon scene of incredible peace. Just as the last rays of the setting sun struck the tops of the sails, the boats lined up as if I'd choreographed them, and I made this photograph of Elephantine Island and the first cataract of the Nile.

PAGES 38–39: *Children, Luxor.* The streets were gaily decorated in honor of the Prophet Muhammed's birthday. When my camera was set up, all the children formed a line directly in front of me in their stiff, ready-to-be-photographed poses. I offered a prize to the child who could run to the green door and get back to me first. The photograph was made as they ran toward me. All received a piece of candy!

PAGES 40–41: *Western Desert and Elephantine Island.* For this sublime view I did not have to trek for great distances through the dunes in unbearable heat, as was true for some scenes. Instead, I was able to capture this desert landscape from the roof of the New Cataract Hotel in Aswan. My only regret is that I forgot to order a gin and tonic from room service. I was on assignment for the *New York Times*, and I'm sure they would have been happy to pay for refreshments.

Sinai

God in his wisdom created the world; we live our lives, passing through time and space, finally departing. The essence of our lives is passage. Everything that we have made will decay; finally, nothing is left. Such were my thoughts when I revisited Sinai last week after two years. Since I was there last, the Egyptians have paved roads that the Israelis had left unpaved, and built new roads that Israel had never considered building. They have built a Holiday Village at Santa Katerina, a large mosque, and they are now working on a massive concrete structure that will be, I suppose, an administrative headquarters. I understand why they might want all these things, but, as I gazed down from Abu-Jiffa onto the valley below, I found myself wishing them gone.

So it was that I came to think of passage. Israel occupied Sinai twice in the last thirty years. Twice it was returned to Egyptian control in the hope of achieving peace. Much of what was built no longer exists: some was bulldozed, a good deal was blown up, and what was simply abandoned is now overshadowed by larger, more numerous Egyptian structures. But as I stood there, I realized that all the buildings would crumble, turn to rubble, then, worn down by rain and sand, to dust borne off by the wind. Some things, of course, crumble more elegantly than others. Concrete buildings seem to fare more poorly than pyramids, which have deteriorated over one or two thousand years. I consoled myself with the thought: everything that had been built, Egyptian and Israeli, would one day become desert sand. The Sinai will have triumphed.

The desert instills a sense of humility. Perhaps that is why most people prefer a more urban environment. God knew what He was doing when He commanded Moses and the Israelites to spend forty years wandering in Sinai. They had a lot of thinking to do. They had seen with their own eyes how well the glory of Pharaoh held up against the power of God. In Sinai, God revealed Himself to man, and the Israelites spent these years understanding the revelation they had witnessed. Every generation, it says in the Passover Haggadah, should see itself as having been redeemed from Egypt. Every generation, I say, should spend some time in Sinai. Our sages teach that a man should make himself like a desert: humble and receptive to guidance from above. No wonder Moses and the Israelites didn't bother to raise monuments to their passage. Nothing merely physical is a monument to divine revelation—not even a monastery. They learned the lesson of Sinai. Other ancient travelers through the region left some graffiti at least. From the ancient Jews, nothing. They understood.

Sinai's grandeur renders human attempts at grandeur pitiful, even silly. Sinai was formerly split in two by a line running arbitrarily from El-Arish in the north to Ras-Muhammed in the south: everything east of the line was Israel, everything west Egypt. The border was marked by barrels whose tops were painted red, the bottoms white. When a barrel was standing with its red side up you were in Israel. When the white side was up, you were in Egypt. Or was it vice-versa? I could never remember. The Bedouin found their own uses for these barrels and moved them at their convenience. What were you to make of a single barrel, standing red-side-up (or worse yet, lying on its side on the ground with neither side up) five kilometers from where the border was supposed to be?

This border was hard to take seriously, so naturally enough I ignored it. This was the kind of border you could find endearing, a demonstration of human frailty, an acknowledgment by both sides that an imaginary line running straight through Sinai, splitting mountains, wadis, trees, even Bedouin families, was wishful thinking. The line might have succeeded as a work of conceptual art, the concept being the transience of human pretension and accomplishment versus the permanence and beauty of Sinai. As art, it cost Sinai nothing. The Bedouin collected the barrels at the end of the project.

Not all art is so innocent. In 1980 I worked in Sinai for two-week stretches, mostly on the Israeli side of the border, but occasionally on the Egyptian side. You were permitted to enter Egyptian Sinai for less than one week at a time, but you could leave and then come back. So I would fly back to Jerusalem each Friday to spend the Sabbath with my family, returning to Sinai Sunday morning. About one o'clock on a Sunday morning, the BBC called me from London. There was a French artist by the name of Jean Verame working on a large project in Egyptian Sinai. He was painting Wadi Nafach, not far from Santa Katerina and Mount Sinai. They wanted pictures. Could I go? I would try, I said, and went back to sleep. At about three o'clock I got another phone call, this one from Larry Thorson of Associated Press. He wanted to come with me; we agreed to meet in Eilat.

When they told me Jean Verame was painting Wadi Nafach, they weren't kidding. I quote from Larry Thorson's AP report published in the *International Herald Tribune* on December 3, 1980:

SINAI BLACK AND BLUE
Mount Sinai, Egypt. With 13 tons of paint, a French artist is well advanced on a plan to paint large expanses of a desert valley near Mount Sinai.

Jean Verame, who calls the work "Sinai Peace Junction," dismisses criticism. "I am a Nature lover," he said. "I destroy nothing. Nature has its dimension and I add a human dimension . . ."

The eye, used to long vistas dominated by subtle tones ranging from tan to rose in the desert mountains, is first riveted to 10 bright blue boulders. Then other sections leap into sight. The flat side of a small stone peak has two blue squares painted on it. On the other side of the valley a rock wall has been painted with a square, solid black except for five brilliant blue boulders.

A boulder here, a boulder there, all in the blue that dominates. And in the center of the valley, which measures about two miles by three [3.2 by 4.8 kilometers], a granite hill rises out of the sand and sagebrush with a kind of loose polka-dot effect, some parts black and some blue . . .

"Sadat said the earth was important to him, sacred," Verame said. "He liked the fact that I wanted to put my work on the earth. Before, the rocks were anonymous."

This wasn't a harmless publicity stunt. He did this not for the sake of some concrete good, such as a Holiday Village, or a desire to provide good health services to the Bedouin, or to build an administrative center for local government, but only to serve his mania for self-aggrandizement. And it cost Sinai a lot.

First he sanded the stones with a blaster, sprayed primer, then finally paint. The Dutch company that supplied the paint guaranteed that it would last at least a hundred years. He lacked all sense of color harmony. The effect, were it pleasing, would have been serious enough. Backed by so-called respectable art institutions worldwide, he had received funding from numerous sources. This was a wonderful stunt for the Dutch paint company, but what excuse could the guardians of the art world give for their support?

At an earlier date, he had tried to get support from Israel for the project, but was sent packing. Now those who cared about Sinai were powerless—they filed reports and protests with conservation groups all over the world. An English group connected with the University of London succeeded in gaining international support from conservation groups for a project designating southern Sinai as an International Peace Park. The U.S. Fish and Wildlife Service set up and funded a program to train Egyptian staff and rangers for the project. And while Egyptians were sent by their government to the United States for training, there is no constituency in Egypt for conservation, no Sierra Club. All programs failed, and we were defeated.

Of course, I knew then in Wadi Nafach that we had no hope of stopping Jean Verame. He was a madman and nearly finished. His project was only a prelude to what would follow under Egyptian administration: blasting coral reefs in order to increase the catch of fish; blasting a new road through the oasis of Ain-Fortaga; excessive development in the Santa Katerina area, which will inevitably lead to pollution of the water table. I'm not claiming that Israel was innocent: Israel began development in Sinai. But public pressure groups in Israel prevented the worst excesses and conducted successful public education programs to increase awareness of the importance of conservation. In Egypt, no one seems to care. True, Israeli tourists left their trash, but it was hauled away. Now Mount Sinai is buried under aluminum cans and candy wrappers.

Today when I go to Sinai, I try to escape as quickly as I can to those wilderness areas where the Egyptians allow me to go. All I have to do is close my eyes until I arrive.

What do you see when you close your eyes? Anything you like, anything you can imagine. Often nothing at all. Try closing your eyes and imagine some natural scene, alpine meadows or a deserted sandy beach. Picture every mountain, boulder, rock, cloud, grain of sand, every tree and flower; make it blow in the wind of your mind: let it rain, cause the seasons to pass, the rock slowly to weather and change; hold every detail, every blade of grass in your imagination, sure in the knowledge of how it began and how it will end. Do this in an instant. This is the work of the Creator. We can't even imagine it, let alone cause it to happen. Nothing can be so fine, so perfect as the beauty of virgin wilderness. Our imagination can summon at best a vague memory centered around a moment. Photography anchors that moment.

My equipment is heavy, and getting it anywhere on foot requires an effort maintained only by single-minded determination. As I climbed from Bikat e-Rabah to the high country, I left Santa Katerina and all its abominations behind me. By the time I'd made it to the top, "Egypt" was nowhere to be found; only Sinai lay before me. The air was clean, a little cool, and silence ruled over all. I had four days in the wilderness ahead of me, we had plenty of food, the wadis were flowing with water, and even the light looked promising.

This was more than I had expected. It was already late April, when, in the often hazy air, clarity of vision over any significant distance is poor. Worse, there are usually few clouds in the sky at this time of year, and Sinai without clouds is like a good steak without pepper. Clouds fill the large sky, cast their shadows across the immense vistas, and add depth to the expanses of monotone. On this trip, I was blessed with clouds in all shapes and sizes, at all times of day. All I had to do was set up my camera and point it in the right direction.

With me on this trip was Shaked, two Bedouin, and a camel. One of the Bedouin was a camel driver, the other a guide named Aouda. We didn't really need a Bedouin guide, but "union regulations" meant we had no choice. Most days, we sent the camel off in the morning to meet us at some predetermined spot later in the day. Camels have broad, padded feet, which make them excellent transport in sandy areas, but less useful for the rocky terrain we were going to be working.

We had begun our hike rather late this first day, what with the drive from Jerusalem and the border crossing, so all of us walked together through Wadi Tubug (page 48) to Aouda's orchard in Wadi Shag, where we spent the night.

Most of the Bedouin have walled orchards in the high country, where they often spend the summer months with their families. Here they enjoy the cool mountain air and abundant fresh fruit in the shade of their trees. We arrived early in the season, and few Bedouin were to be seen. So we had this paradise almost entirely to ourselves, and I felt, as I walked along from garden to garden, much as Adam must have felt in Eden. The whole world was mine to enjoy, without any need of exclusive possession. A place like Sinai belongs to those who love it.

After the night in Aouda's garden, we set off, without the camel, for the area around Jebel Babb. From the inside looking out, his garden had seemed large and luxuriant. From one hundred meters, it was a small island of green in an arid desert. But even from a distance of several kilometers, such small oases draw your attention and hold your imagination (pages 62–63). Inside the walls of one of these gardens, you dream of roaming through the mountains. As you roam, your eye instinctively seeks shelter.

Sitting at home in Jerusalem, looking at photographs awakens my wanderlust. Even a map will suffice to spark my imagination; one map or another is almost always pinned to my bulletin board. It may be a place I visited long ago, like Norway's Rondane Mountains, or a place I've never been to and to which I am not likely to go, Iraq or Saudi Arabia, say. Alaska, Yosemite, or Haleakala Crater in Hawaii excite similar emotions: all are wilderness, all represent in my mind freedom and beauty. Yet Sinai is the most inviting of all. It is the most familiar, and familiarity breeds affection. Sinai is a real wilderness, almost without limit when you're on foot, rugged and wild, untamed.

That morning when we left Aouda's garden, we were headed to Jebel Babb, one of the wilder areas of Sinai. You climb until you reach a sort of plateau—sort of, since it's far from flat—and you walk through a wide *farsh* (Arabic for mattress), open in all directions. This is a pleasant place to be, for the walking is easy and you always have an inviting expanse in front of you, beckoning toward the horizon. The problem is that the horizon surrounds you, and no matter which way you go, you wish to go the other way, because the view promises to be good from there, too. As you can't be everywhere at once, even as you walk, you're already longing to return—a nostalgia for the present. This is one of the rare times in life when the present, not some idealized image of the past or future, is so sweet that you can taste it: delight, desire, satisfaction, and longing experienced all at the same moment.

After a *farsh* it is either up or down, and we climbed up through the mountains to yet another *farsh*, this one smaller and higher than the last. It was strewn with fantastic granite boulders scattered about as my son scatters toys across the floor of his room. This *farsh* didn't merely promise horizons: it delivered them. Walking around and even climbing under these massive boulders, you would all of a sudden glimpse the nearby mountain peaks, polished granite surfaces glittering in the sun. Along the way, I made several photographs of the surrounding mountains: Jebel Katerina, Jebel Mugasseb, Jebel Umm-

Shummar, Jebel Abu-Shajara, Jebel Tarboosh (pages 66–67). As we climbed up Jebel Mugasseb in order to obtain a view of Jebel Babb (*babb* means gate) and the adjoining Babb El-Duniya, I labored under the weight of my backpack containing my 4x5 view camera. Aouda came and took it from me, slinging it over his back. It felt as if I had grown wings. After a few meters, Aouda said: "No wonder your pack is so heavy. The whole world is in it! Jebel Katerina, Jebel Umm-Shummar . . ." Atlas should have been a photographer.

We climbed up the granite dome of Jebel Mugasseb; the thought of other granite domes I had climbed long ago in Yosemite came to me. One of Yosemite's lesser domes, Pywiack, was some 550 meters higher than Jebel Mugasseb, and it was not quite above the tree line in the High Sierra of California. There, in California, instead of a rock-filled *farsh* of scattered low bushes, were grassy meadows and cliffs dotted with evergreen trees. Here, in Sinai, each blade of grass is a small miracle, and, standing on my windy dome, you would have had to search with binoculars to find a tree. But that is how I have come to like my landscapes, without trees to block the views. A tree here and there adds a bit of flavor, especially if it is a windblown cypress, but these absolutely naked landscapes have a way of growing on you.

From Jebel Mugasseb looking east, you could see its near neighbor Jebel Babb, and following the ridge of Jebel Babb to the right, the Babb El-Duniya, Gate to the World. Babb El-Duniya was a small V, a narrow gate that opened onto the promise of a magnificent view of the area blocked by the ridge. It was getting late, so we decided to save Babb El-Duniya for the next day and began our descent through Wadi Za'atar to Farsh Rumana, where our camel was waiting.

We awoke the next morning to a thick fog and gray, cloudy skies. It seemed certain it would be a rainy day, if not a snowy one. We crawled back into our sleeping bags; in that heavy mist, it was insane to think of climbing higher. But by the time we had finally arisen, not so very much later, the fog was burning off, and there were patches of blue in the sky. We prepared to ascend to Babb El-Duniya, about an hour and a half from where we were camped. By the time we climbed via a canyonlike wadi to the *farsh* above us, the skies were completely blue; a slight haze hovered over the more distant peaks. We had just started to strip off our coats when the first massive clouds sailed toward us. Despite the light haze that hindered visibility, the clouds looked like they would provide some interest. I was hopeful.

As we climbed slowly up to the crest, the view opened up before us. First the mountaintops directly in front, then Wadi Abu-Jedidah far below us, pointing the way to the West and Egypt. We could just make out the Gulf of Suez glimmering in the distance, but the haze was too thick to permit a clear photograph. Over the short range, we had a fairly clear view of Jebel Madsus and Jebel Tarboosh (pages 70–71). The rapidly shifting shadow areas made the scene attractive, despite the haze, and gave me reason to believe I might do some nice work. Standing so high up, watching the immense cloud shadows race across vast stretches of landscape, I thought the mountains were leaping from light to shadow and back again. In the midst of a world in movement, we sat secure on our boulders, listening to the wind and eating chocolate and oranges. Who ever remembers that this entire world is rolling and twisting through space? At Babb El-Duniya we sat on the very edge of the world, conscious of that fact—aware, too, that security is an illusion, but secure nonetheless. As we headed back, a few drops of rain fell on our heads, to remind us that anything could happen at any time.

Sinai is the kind of place where you'll find whatever you're looking for, according to your sensitivity and perception. From a small distance you could easily pass by some wonder. It was Mordi, my assistant and guide for the first year I worked in Sinai, who had to point out the things I had failed to notice, often doing so with some exasperation at my insensitivity. For example: the low mound of stones—nearly two meters long with a small opening on one end and closed on the other—I walked by without comment. It was a leopard trap fashioned by men of long ago. They would bait it with meat near the closed end. The trap was just big enough for a leopard to wriggle into. When he had seized the meat and shook it once or twice, as leopards will do, he also tugged at a rope tied to the meat and attached to a small rock placed over a slit in the roof of the trap. As he tugged, the flat rock would come crashing down behind him. The men waiting nearby could then leap out and kill the leopard, thrusting spears through holes in the side and top of the trap. Leopards have been gone from Sinai for some years, but we are now sighting them more often in the Judean Desert as they make their way south again. One day they may return to Sinai.

You could also find bits and pieces of all sorts of things, and, as we drove through the wadis, Mordi would suddenly stop the Jeep to collect a piece of rope, metal, or an old inner tube, tossing it into the back so it would be there when we needed it. The inner tubes he cut into slices, attaching all the little loops together to make a long piece of rubber that could be used to secure some piece of equipment.

The collecting disease was contagious; I learned to keep my eyes peeled for the odd shiny object. We once set out in the Jeep for a two-week trip, and it was only when we were well into some sandy wadi that I remembered I had brought just one, nearly empty, box of matches and no pen. Both were critical: without matches, no pipe-smoking and no hot food; without a pen, no record of the photographs. We camped that evening in Wadi Arada and, after we had carefully built a fire using only one match, we lit our pipes from the embers, and I set out for a moonlight stroll. Twenty or thirty meters from the campsite, a glitter on the ground caught my eye. There was a Parker pen and, next to it, a box of matches. The

matches were dry, and the pen worked. Just try and find a pen that works when you need one! My wife used it for years and was inordinately upset when she finally lost it, no doubt to be found by someone else in urgent need of a working pen.

Sometimes you find something too big to put in your pocket or even a Jeep. Suppose you come across a lovely little mountain with no name? If no one who came before you thought to name it, then why not do so yourself? It belongs to you more than anyone else. Sinai belongs to those who love it, and the names I chose were with this in mind.

For me, Sinai is divided into three areas: granite, sandstone, and the coast. Granite is a hard rock, often found in the higher altitudes; it weathers into jagged forms. The high country around Jebel Katerina is nearly all granite. Sandstone is soft, readily sculpted by wind and water into unusual forms that are rounder and lower than the granite areas. The coastal areas are, of course, close to sea level and are sometimes characterized by long stretches of sandy beach leading gently down to the water; sometimes there are cliffs and rocks at water's edge. Each area has its own character.

Most of my work between 1980 and 1982 was in the sandstone areas, so it was sandstone I came to know best. During these years, the granite areas, concentrated in western Sinai, were under Egyptian control, and the sandstone and eastern coastal areas were in Israel. Mordi and I roamed freely through Israeli territory, and it was amid the sculpted sandstone mountains of southern Sinai that I first grappled with the problems of scale and mood I discussed in the introduction.

On our first trip together in 1980, Mordi and I headed down from the coast to Santa Katerina on an unpaved road textured like corrugated metal. The road was fairly level until it reached a narrow pass and then made a rapid descent into a large sandstone valley. To the left was a sandstone hill, an old truck atop it with big white numbers painted on the side, "1956," a memorial to the

1956 Sinai campaign; to the right, a broad open valley that via Wadi Razala led to the large oasis of Ain-Fortaga, where the Egyptians are now blasting a new road. Then, above the oasis of Ain-Khudra, Inscription Rock, a sandstone boulder inscribed with the graffiti of ancient pilgrims perhaps returning from Mecca or going to Mount Sinai through the Valley of Pilgrims. A Bedouin ranger hired by the Israel Nature Reserve Authority used to sit there to make sure that none of the thousands of modern visitors defaced it. Now, though few people visit, it has been defaced by modern graffiti. Perhaps it is better that modern travelers should continue the ancient tradition, maybe it is simply a shame. We continued rattling and hopping down the road, making a sudden left turn into a small wadi. There Mordi parked the Jeep near a small acacia tree, and we set about collecting firewood.

Rising early next morning, we drove to *nawamis*, a collection of ancient burial huts perched on a hill. All are made of local stone, with a roof of one large, flat stone and a single opening to the west. These *nawamis* are found on various sites in Sinai, but this is the largest grouping in one place. After I'd made some photographs, we were again on our way, driving roughly south at breakneck speed through sand-filled wadis. In soft sand, you must either go very slowly in "front special" (low gear, 4-wheel drive) or very fast in "front" (high gear, 4-wheel drive) to keep from sinking. There is a unique pleasure in driving this way through sand: it is something of an art, and, moreover, it is fun to be moving so fast in a sandy, deserted wadi. If you choose the wrong moment to change gears, you suddenly find yourself motionless and axle-deep in sand. Going uphill in sand is also quite a challenge. Here the trick is to make a running start at high speed and try to get up the hill without changing gears. Of course, just as you approach the crest, you have to be alert and stop or risk flying off into space, as Mordi did once with a Jeep belonging to the Israel Society for the Protection of Nature.

Mordi and I headed south through the sands to Bikat Baraka. How shall I describe the place? Every once in a while I look at it in one of the photographs on my living-room wall and go through a memory exercise: the route to Bikat Baraka, the places we camped, the layout of the area. It's like remembering the face of a friend. In my mind, I trudge through the sand dunes, look back at my footprints in the smooth sand, and watch the sand blow gently just above the surface of the dunes. All this I can see clearly. It is part of my memory. Once I spent a few days photographing the operations of an old yacht converted to a pilot boat in California. We were anchored halfway between the Golden Gate and the Farallon Islands, waiting to greet approaching ships. For weeks after, I dreamed of the sea and its motion. Just so with Bikat Baraka, a sea of sand in gentle motion (page 86).

It is the essence of the desert, for it has no trees, no water, nothing but sand and sandstone. It isn't on the route to anywhere. Bedouin don't come here, for they are a practical people and have no need of this place. It has the flavor of wind and dust.

When the wind blows hard enough, it raises the sand and dust until it pelts you in the face, coming, it seems, from all sides. The sand, being heavier, remains close to the surface and, on the side of a sand dune, forms waves. A flat area becomes as smooth as glass, obliterating all texture. On such a day, I donned goggles and set out from the Jeep with camera and tripod in hand. At eye level the dust bombarded me, but, looking up, I saw that the sky was surprisingly clear. At ground level, the sand moved so quickly that my footprints were erased almost instantly. It was a strange sensation to be standing in the midst of sand, all trace of my approach obliterated, as if I'd been dropped from the heavens. A small sandstone hill to the east caught my eye; it and a pebble were the only objects at close range that remained static. Above it, blue sky. The photograph made (page 87), I retreated to the Jeep, and

I drove until I found shelter from the sandstorm in a small bitter-water oasis in Wadi Baraka.

Bikat Baraka was on the way to nowhere. Imagine our surprise, then, when one day Mordi and I were driving along the western side and came across a lone French hippie, on foot. He didn't wave, but we stopped. "Where are you going?" we asked. "To the Egyptian border." When we asked if he had a map, he pulled out a small map of Israel with Sinai tucked into a little box at the bottom. This was like crossing the ocean on an air mattress. Did he have water? He held up and shook a half-filled canteen. Food? A can of fish. Did he want help? No!

He was as good as dead. It was already getting dark, rain clouds were building up, and though he was—incredibly—heading more or less in the right direction, he would surely lose his way in the approaching twilight and never be seen again. He had some twenty kilometers ($12\frac{1}{2}$ miles) to go before coming to water and a main road. We opened the door to the Jeep and motioned him in: he didn't want to come until we promised to take him to the border immediately. We dropped him off at the Israeli border outpost, leaving him with the bewildered officials. He didn't thank us or wave good-bye as we drove off.

Some two months later, I read a notice in the paper about a French tourist who had disappeared in Sinai. If he had been seeking oblivion, he was on the right path.

Not that I haven't been lost, or at least temporarily misplaced. On one of my trips with Aryeh Shimron, we had decided to cross on foot from the main road south of Dahab to a point on the coast, a distance of ten kilometers through the mountains (if it were possible to travel in a straight line). From there, we would have had to walk another ten kilometers north along the coast to the point where our Jeep could meet us. So we sent our driver off with instructions to meet us that evening and set off. The maps of the area were scanty, but we had aerial survey photographs. We had a difficult climb scrambling up a

little wadi to get over the crest of the first mountain, but after that, all was downhill—theoretically. We found the wadi we were looking for, which we hoped to follow to the coast. After working our way down a small cliff face by means of a few precarious foot- and handholds, we were down in the wadi. The descent was especially difficult for me, since I was carrying a heavy pack with a camera, which put my center of balance behind me. Though I was the only one with a pack, we each had a canteen and some light snacks. Carmel, one of the assistants, was carrying five liters of water. This was careless planning: each of us should have had several liters of water, not to mention adequate food and warm clothing.

It was a pleasant walk down the wadi, and we came occasionally to a small drop, where there would have been a waterfall, had there been water. These falls were not visible on our aerial photographs. We climbed down the falls or found some other way around them.

At one point, I stopped to make a photograph while the others continued. They promised to wait for me under the first shady tree they found. When I was done, I continued walking in the wadi for quite some distance. I had lost their trail, though I was certain I was following the same wadi. Where had they gone?

The sensible thing was to retrace my footsteps to the point where they'd left me. When they missed me, that's where they'd look. I sat down to wait. Around me was silence; the longer I sat there, the more frightening the silence. Then I heard someone shouting, "Neil, Neil, we're over here!" Where? No one was to be seen. I wandered about a little, looking into adjoining small wadis. Perhaps they'd found some shade and water. But no one was around, and I dared not wander far. Then I spotted a figure on the hill opposite, and when I'd climbed it, I saw them all below. Rather than follow the twisting wadi, they climbed. We had been separated by only a small distance.

Reunited, we stayed closer to one another as we made our way through the wadi. As the shadows grew longer and the coast was nowhere to be seen, it became clear that we were going to spend the night here. It was truly lovely as the wadi narrowed, its surface becoming polished granite. We even found some water left from the last rain. It was covered with slime, but nevertheless good, and we filled our canteens.

By this point, the wadi had become a canyon. We soon came to a drop of perhaps fifty meters. There was no way down and no way around.

This was not a feasible route to the sea. The only solution was to climb over mountain ridges until we found another wadi that would lead us out. We climbed two ridges of loose granite, scrambling up, then down the other side. We chose a campsite, protected from the wind, and began collecting wood, for the sky was growing dark. Though it was winter, it was unseasonably warm—lucky for us, since only I had even a light jacket. We built a fire, ate what we had, and each looked for a comfortable niche in which to sleep. Finding a small hole with an overhanging rock, I crawled in and went to sleep. The rock, warm from the heat it had absorbed all day, radiated its warmth through most of the night.

We woke the next morning to the noise of a small plane, which was followed by that of a helicopter. The army was searching for us. We heard them and even caught glimpses of them, but they failed to see us, specks in a wilderness. We found a wadi that looked to be heading in the right direction and seemed big enough to lead to the coast. It led to a small oasis, where the water was too salty to drink, but, clearly, we were close to the coast, and we knew exactly where we were: Moyet Shagara in Wadi Shagarat. As we climbed down toward the coast, a helicopter passed overhead, close enough that we could see the pilot. We waved and shouted and jumped, but he did not see us until we were trudging toward the mouth of the sandy wadi. The pilot landed. They checked us for dehydration and put us on board for a flight to Dahab.

The next morning, as I was leaving Eilat on the drive north to Jerusalem, I picked up a hitchhiking soldier. "You look tired," I observed. He grumbled, "We were up all night the night before last looking for some idiotic geologists who got lost." He slept all the way to Jerusalem.

Shortly after the western half of Sinai had been returned to Egypt, President Navon of Israel visited Egypt and was promised the liberalization of border-crossing procedures between Israeli and Egyptian Sinai. The week after his visit, Shaked and I decided to see what this meant and drove to the Santa Katerina airport, hoping to cross in the Jeep. To our great surprise, the Egyptians let us through, but we were allowed to drive only as far as Santa Katerina. Still, this was something. We stayed the maximum of five days and left, planning to return the next Sunday.

When that day came, we drove up to the border and asked for the officer who had been so friendly with us last week, Captain Muhammed. The soldiers told us to sit down and wait: Captain Muhammed, they said, would be with us shortly. We made ourselves optimistically comfortable in the departure lounge. Half an hour passed and no Captain Muhammed. We flagged down one of the soldiers passing by and inquired after the welfare of our friend. "He's expected any minute. He's just returning from the dentist at Santa." And so he appeared, right on cue, his lower jaw swollen and tied with a white bandage. "Captain Muhammed," I said, "sorry to see you in pain! We'd like to drive to Santa Katerina." He mumbled something unintelligible and shook his head and his finger in unison, signifying NO! "Why not?" I asked. He smiled and whipped out a long handwritten paper in Arabic, Hebrew, English, and French labeled "NEW REGULATIONS." These included the following:

1) A compulsory "development tax" of $5 per person.
2) A ban on entering Sinai in a vehicle brought from Israel.

3) An injunction that travelers take Egyptian transport from the airport to the monastery (the only permitted destination) at $12 apiece. As this is a distance of less than twenty kilometers (12½ miles), it worked out to $1/mile.

Our protests and exclamations of disappointment met with a sympathetic bandaged smile and silence. A true Egyptian, he sat us down and brought us tea to soften the blow. After prolonged negotiations, he eventually agreed that, after we paid the taxes and transport charges, we might be allowed to stay in the Santa Katerina area for four days and three nights, and not necessarily at the monastery. Did this include hiking in the area? He allowed that we might be permitted to hike and sleep on Jebel Musa (Mount Sinai) and its neighboring peak, Jebel Safsafa, for the entire period. So now all we had to do was wait for the next bus to Santa Katerina. We unloaded all the equipment from the Jeep, leaving it in Captain Muhammed's personal care, and waited for the bus.

They were really very sorry, but as the new regulations were *very new* there was as yet no bus service. But they would find a Bedouin to take us in his truck. Some time later we were bouncing up and down in the back of an open truck for only $1 per person per mile. We had stepped through the looking glass; we stopped on the way to visit with Mad Jean Verame at Peace Junction. The impression he made on us in his goggles, blue-spotted sneakers, and overalls, wielding his spray gun in the midst of a Sinai wadi, fit in well with everything we had experienced that day.

Departing from Peace Junction, we were dropped at the foot of Mount Sinai. After making an appointment with our driver to return for us at ten o'clock four days later, we hired a camel to carry the equipment and food. There were five of us altogether, the Bedouin camel driver, David (my wife's cousin, who was visiting Israel), Shaked, Larry Thorson (the AP bureau chief from Israel), and I. Larry had come with us to

visit Wadi Nafach, where Jean Verame was remaking the desert in his image, but as Larry was such good company, we prevailed upon him to stay with us for the rest of the trip. After that, he often joined our expeditions. As we prepared to depart, a Bedouin friend of Shaked's came over to visit with him and ask after his health. When Shaked complained that his back ached, the Bedouin ran over to his home and brought back with him a *lazgaz*, Arabic for back plaster. It was a genuine Johnson & Johnson® American Medicated Back Plaster, as large as this page. The unfolded wings of an American bald eagle graced the package, with instructions in Arabic below. We took it and set off.

We had some lovely days exploring the *farshes* of Jebel Safsafa and climbing the summit of Jebel Musa to watch the sunrise. Shaked's back was not troubling him, I made some nice photographs, and the only problem, aside from the garbage that had been collecting on this Holy Mountain since the last garbage collection just before the Israeli withdrawal, was that Larry had forgotten to bring a sleeping bag. The nights were cool but not cold, and I had one of those emergency space blankets that have a texture like Saran Wrap™ and a finish like aluminum foil. Every night, as we gathered around our little fire to enjoy its warmth, Larry would wrap himself in the space blanket and sit there glowing and crinkling like a roasting turkey. (I know he will forgive me for this description.)

On the last day, we started our descent early. As we walked, Shaked's back began to ache. We had to stop and massage him almost every ten minutes on the way down. Arriving just at ten o'clock at the appointed meeting place, we saw coming toward us a small miracle: a bus. The Egyptians had, after all, provided the bus service promised in the "new regulations," for which we had paid so dearly. It was the last thing we had expected to see. We climbed in and sat near the back of the nearly empty bus, which contained, aside from the driver, only one other person, a neat Egyptian gentleman in a suit and tie, who introduced himself as the assistant to the Egyptian minister of tourism.

We expected to be whisked directly to the airport, but there was an unscheduled stop at the monastery to pick up a group of German tourists. All we had to do was wait until they finished their tour. So we sat and waited. When finally all thirty of them made their way to the bus and had taken their seats, we made a halting start, building up speed slowly until we reached our cruising speed and were almost ready to begin our descent to the Santa Katerina airport. At this point, the bus lost speed and ground to a halt.

The driver got out for a look-see, and we sat some more. We did finally reach the airport some two and one half hours after we had boarded the bus. Shaked had been sitting uncomfortably in the same position for the entire period, and when it came time to go, he couldn't move. He was stuck in a sitting position. As carefully as we could, David, Larry, the assistant to the Egyptian minister of tourism, and I lifted him, in a sitting position, out of his seat and stretched him out, belly down, on a blanket spread on the airport runway under the wide-eyed stares of thirty German tourists. Then I remembered the back plaster and was trying to figure out how to apply it, when our Egyptian official came over and said, "Please permit me. I also suffer from back problems."

Yielding to a greater expertise, I gave him the back plaster, and he pulled down Shaked's pants, half exposing my friend's buttocks. The Egyptian applied the plaster, exclaiming as he did so: "Bismallah!" which means, "In the name of Allah!"

When I began working in Sinai, I hadn't pictured such an inglorious conclusion: a backache, a plaster, and a bare behind among a busload of tourists. It would be nice if Sinai could always remain the pristine wilderness that it is in my photographs. Far more glorious if my memories allowed me always to remain at Babb El-Duniya, eating chocolate and oranges at the edge of the world. But, as Shaked and I raced back to Israel from our most recent trip to Santa Katerina in my Ford Escort (Jeeps are now forbidden to enter Egypt from Israel) along the newly paved road down to the coast, my heart ached at the large blue signs: "FOREIGNERS ARE FORBIDDEN TO LEAVE THE MAIN ROAD." Imagine seeing someone you love, whom you haven't seen for years, through a pane of thick glass that forbids touch and prevents communication, save that of longing.

We have done all we can to draw the world's attention to the state of affairs in Sinai; but the Egyptians have shown by their lack of action that conservation in Sinai is a low priority for them. They have, I know, more immediate problems. But with international assistance, they've undertaken huge restoration projects for the antiquities in the Nile Valley, projects beautifully and skillfully implemented, as any visitor to Egypt has noted. These antiquities draw thousands of visitors annually, from all over the world. The Sinai is a treasure no less important than the pyramids or the Temple of Abu-Simbel. I speak out at the risk of losing the privilege of visiting Sinai, but I owe Sinai that much. And now I am perhaps the only person in a position to publicize the problem. I call for the creation of a protected wilderness area in southern Sinai, to be designated an International Peace Park, run along the lines of America's national parks.

Sinai must be preserved.

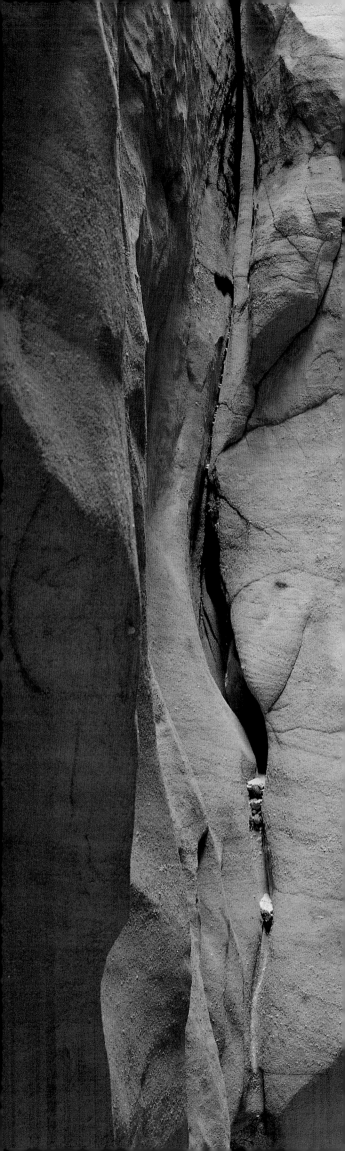

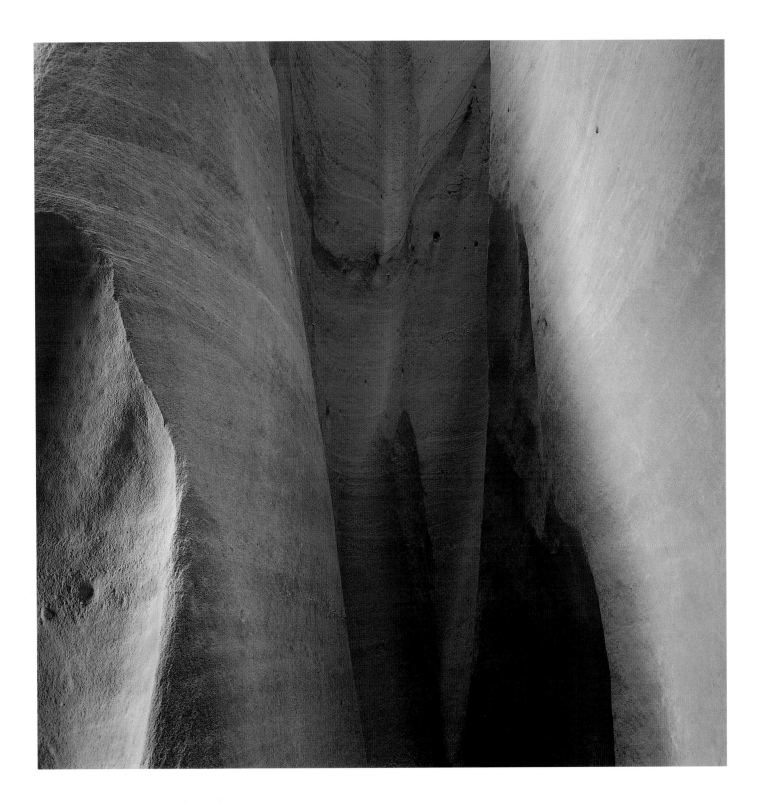

PAGE 43: *Canyon of Colors.*

PAGES 44–45: *View from the summit of Jebel Musa.* The question of whether or not the summit from which this photograph was made is actually Mount Sinai always seems to me to be irrelevant. It offers one of the finer views in southern Sinai.

PAGE 46: *Isle of Tiran, evening.* Mordi and I came out of the wadi that led us to the coast to Ganei-El-Rayan just as the sky was darkening to a deep blue. It was such a lovely scene that Mordi instinctively sought a better view and drove up to the top of a little hill. Working quickly to set up the camera, I made this exposure of almost two minutes, which was long enough for the fast-moving clouds to blur. The Isle of Tiran was used as a base by the Egyptians to prevent Israeli ships from entering the gulf on their way to Eilat. This action precipitated the Six-Day War.

PAGE 48: *Bedouin orchard, Wadi Tubug.* For years I had thought this walled orchard was located in Wadi Jibal, but on a recent hike through there, I discovered the orchard was not there at all. I found it in Wadi Tubug, and the trees were blooming with white flowers, but I'd already used my last sheet of film and couldn't make a photograph. For now, I'll have to be satisfied with the memory.

PAGE 51: *Santa Katerina from Abu-Jiffa.*

PAGE 55: *Garden of Hassan Musa, Wadi Jibal.*

PAGE 58: *Jebel Katerina and the High Country.* From the sandstone areas in eastern Sinai.

PAGE 61: *Santa Katerina in snowstorm.* My wife, Anna, came with me on this trip in the winter of 1979. Snowflakes were falling on our car as we arrived in Santa Katerina, and it continued snowing during the night. We had intended to make an overnight hike into the mountains, but the weather caused us to scale down our plans and we decided to take a walk through Wadi Ain-Arba'in. We got as far as the mouth of the wadi, where this photograph was made. By the time I'd finished photographing the fast-moving clouds and the stormy light, we were so cold that we had to return to the field school.

PAGES 62–63: *Bedouin gardens in Wadi Shag.* Despite the difficulties of living in this environment, these gardens offer a person everything he really needs: shelter, water, and food. In an environment wholly of man's making it is possible to have the illusion of complete independence from all natural forces. Wilderness can be a place where self-reliance is the only hope of survival, but it is also a place where the limits of one's ability are clearly revealed. Without constant care and attention, the wilderness will swallow these islands of green.

PAGES 64–65: *Monastery of Santa Katerina.* Here the monastery can be seen in its proper perspective, dwarfed by the grandeur of its surroundings.

PAGES 66–67: *Jebel Umm-Shummar from Jebel Babb.* These are the granite mountains of the High Country at their grandest: peak after peak, culminating in Jebel Umm-Shummar. It looks deceptively like the European Alps, but the granite is the red granite of Sinai and there is not a tree to be seen.

PAGE 68: *Olive tree in Wadi Talab.* I made this photograph on my first trip to Santa Katerina, in 1979. At that time, Shaked was director of the Israeli Field Study Center at Santa Katerina and Mordi was working there as a guide. He suggested daily excursions for me, arranging Bedouin guides and a camel to carry the equipment. I recall being surprised at the quantity of water and greenery found in these high mountain wadis. The arid surroundings only sharpen the beauty of this idyllic scene.

PAGE 69: *Pool and rock, Wadi Talab.* I usually avoid photographing small details like this, which could be anywhere and give little impression of their environment. Nevertheless, some things are too beautiful to pass by, such as this perfectly round rock in a crystal clear pool.

PAGES 70–71: *Jebel Tarboosh from Babb El-Duniya.* "Standing so high up, watching the immense cloud shadows race across vast stretches of landscape, I thought the mountains were leaping from light to shadow and back again. In the midst of a world in movement, we sat secure on our boulders, listening to the wind and eating chocolate and oranges. Who ever remembers that this entire world is rolling and twisting through space? At Babb El-Duniya we sat on the very edge of the world, conscious of that fact—and aware, too, that security is an illusion, but secure nonetheless."

PAGES 72–73: *Panorama from Jebel Marwa to Freia.* Shortly after Sinai had been returned to Egypt, I came to the Santa Katerina area with two friends intending to hike. We hired a camel and guide from the sheikh, after a bit of bargaining, and set off. We made camp in a two-room Bedouin hut, which by the evening had filled with other Bedouin. My two friends, somewhat wary, went to sit in the other room, while I remained with the Bedouin, who were chatting around the fire, singing, and idly sharpening their knives to while away the time. As we began to discuss the arrangements for the next day, it became clear that we had misunderstood each other: they expected to be paid on a daily basis, while I had intended to pay them for three days. We began to shout at each other, and one of my friends came out to see what the commotion was about. The first and only thing he noticed was the argument and the knife sharpening, and he ran out of the door into the blackness of the snowstorm. He could have been hopelessly lost in three minutes, and an icicle by morning, so we all ran out after him, finally convincing him that the argument was not all that serious. Nevertheless, since I hadn't the money to pay their price, we decided to return the next morning. I rose early and made this photograph before we departed.

PAGES 74–75: *Wadi Zawatin and Jebel Katerina.* In the harshness of the surroundings, these olive trees (*zawatin* are olives) offer the promise of shade and water. In the distance is Jebel Katerina, the highest mountain in Sinai, with a small white church on its summit.

PAGE 76: *Dunes and Jebel Zakuf, Bikat Baraka.* As we drove into this sandstorm, we had to resist the urge to seek shelter from the sand pelting us from all sides. Despite the unpleasantness, it was a beautiful scene: all forms were softened by the blowing sand, and all distant detail was obscured. Nothing seemed real, save the rippled dune directly in front of us.

PAGE 77: *Oasis at Bir-Biriya.* Certainly one of the smallest oases in Sinai, this one nevertheless has all the essentials: water, shade, and swarms of flies.

PAGES 78–79: *Jebel Zakuf, Bikat Baraka.* This was the first photograph I made in Sinai that seemed to capture its essence. It was a heavily overcast day, with no hint of a break in the clouds. Nevertheless, I set up my camera and waited for a long time, hoping for a burst of brilliant light. When it came, it lasted just long enough to make one photograph. Mordi and I celebrated with a glass of whiskey.

PAGES 80–81: *Canyon of Wadi Arada Hagadol.* Canyons like these are not unique to Sinai and may be found in sandstone areas all over the world. Once having entered a canyon, you are compelled to follow it until the end, or until you can no longer squeeze through. At that point, you might look up to find that the canyon extends farther, but that to continue you will have to shimmy up a chimney, bracing and supporting yourself against opposite walls. The walls are sometimes "painted" with fantastic colors and forms, like those of the Canyon of Colors.

PAGE 82: *Sandstone, Wadi Arada HaKatan.* The small rocks that have fallen off the face of this ledge are a reminder of the process of change and erosion in the desert. I recall once walking through a narrow wadi under overhanging rocks. One day, I thought, something will fall. Beyond the next bend lay a camel, crushed under a large boulder, only its feet sticking out.

PAGE 83: *Canyon of Wadi Arada Hagadol.* See above, pages 80–81.

PAGE 84: *Hamadat El-Loz.* This is a low area between Jebel Matamir and Jebel Ikry that we valued as a secluded campsite, not far off the Jeep track to Bikat Baraka. No one ever came through here. It is a lovely place, whose only sound is silence.

PAGE 85: *Jebel Matamir and Jebel Ikry.* This is a view from the eastern side of Jebel Matamir looking toward its western half and near neighbor, Jebel Ikry. The low area between the two mountains is part of Hamadat El-Loz.

PAGE 86: *Great Dune and clouds, Bikat Baraka.* This dune rises from Wadi Adudeh to the eastern edge of Bikat Baraka and extends for quite a distance. The ridge at the top of the dune looks as sharp as a knife. In the morning, after the winds have been blowing all night, the surface of the dune is smooth and delightful to walk on—though you can't help feeling sorry for having destroyed the perfect surface. Through the cleft of the dunes, a distant mountain peak is visible.

PAGE 87: *Sandstorm, Bikat Baraka.* "At ground level, the sand moved so quickly that my footprints were erased almost instantly. It was a strange sensation to be standing in the midst of sand, all trace of my approach obliterated, as if I'd been dropped from the heavens. A small sandstone hill to the east caught my eye: it and a pebble were the only objects at close range that remained static. Above it, blue sky. The photograph made, I retreated to the Jeep, and we drove until we found shelter from the sandstorm in a small bitter-water oasis in Wadi Baraka."

PAGES 88–89: *Oasis of Ain-Khudra.* Ain-Khudra is surrounded on three sides by high, varicolored sandstone walls. Descending from Inscription Rock, not far off the road from the coast to Santa Katerina, I made this photograph as I approached the oasis.

PAGES 90–91: *Haze over mountains, area of Wadi Umm-Hagaban.* The haze was so thick that it was impossible to photograph anything but the haze itself, but the light is as much the subject in a good photograph as any object.

PAGES 92–93: *Wadi Mandar, early evening.* Acacia trees have long, sharp thorns that can easily puncture a tire, and every time we came here we could count on at least one flat. We of course carried the tools to fix flats, but it's a rough job on tires as big as a Jeep's. One day we had three flats! Dotted along its entire length with groves of acacia trees, Wadi Mandar is among the broadest in Sinai. The bluish light of the evening sky imparts its color to the bed of the wadi, but a trace of red from the setting sun remains on the little hill in the middle of the wadi.

PAGES 94–95: *View from Jebel Abu-Yahud.* Shaked came to this area with a group on a camel trek. Knowing I would like it, he brought me at the first possible opportunity. This is an area of low granite hills, whose forms echo those of the high granite mountains around Jebel Katerina. In order to make the photograph we ascended this small mountain three times in two days.

PAGE 96: *Red Sea coast at Ras Abu-Galum.* Ras Abu-Galum is a natural lagoon enclosed by coral reefs. We were able to drive the Jeep out onto the spit of land from where this photograph was made. The lovely colors are a result of the coral beneath the nearly transparent water.

PAGE 97: *Acacia and black dike, Wadi Ara'im.* Dikes are intrusions of molten magma that run for vast stretches through certain areas of Sinai. On this trip through the Wadi Kid area, Aryeh Shimron was looking for the junction between two land masses, and I was looking for photographs. He found what he was looking for and so did I—in this back-lit acacia set against a black dike in a little wadi near the end of Wadi Kid.

PAGES 98–99: *Wadi Hweit and Red Sea.* We often camped below this site in Wadi Hweit on our way to and from Sinai, as it is a lovely place just a little off the main road. I had many times ascended the hill to look at the view of the coast, but the sky always seemed empty without clouds.

PAGE 100: *Coral Island, Gulf of Eilat.* This island is just a bit south of Eilat, and the name "Coral Island" is a misnomer, as is the name currently in use by the Egyptians, "Pharoah's Island." The fortress was built by Crusaders and has been undergoing restoration since this photograph was made.

Jordan

The journey began with a drive of fifty kilometers (31 miles) west of my home in Jerusalem. Had I driven ninety kilometers (56 miles) to the east, I would have been in Amman, capital of Jordan. Instead, I flew from Tel Aviv to the island of Cyprus, and from there to Amman, a total air distance of some seven hundred kilometers (434¾ miles). Politics makes for much indirection.

Nearly six months of planning had gone into this journey to the land east of Israel. I was somewhat concerned about how the Jordanians would receive me and decided to seek advice from the American ambassador to Israel, Thomas Pickering, who had previously served as ambassador to Jordan for four and a half years.

To my great surprise, a meeting with the ambassador was easily arranged. His secretary didn't even need a reason. The United States sends their best diplomats to Israel, and Ambassador Pickering is a gem. A tall, hardy-looking man, he's the sort who likes to get out and about. He loves the Middle East and its deserts—having hiked through many of them—and is especially expert in matters of archaeology. As I showed the ambassador my photographs in his Tel Aviv office, I told him about this book and how it had grown from its Sinai heart to include Egypt proper, the Judean wilderness, and Jerusalem. For a long time, I told him, I had dreamed of visiting Jordan, most especially the ancient Nabatean city of Petra, but the obstacles had seemed overwhelming. Now that I was about to realize the achievement of another dream, a comprehensive book of my work in the Middle East, I wanted it be as complete as present political circumstances would allow. Syria, Lebanon, Iraq, and Saudi Arabia were out of the question, but Jordan struck me as a feasible proposition. Ambassador Pickering agreed with me: not only was a visit feasible, but it would be a major omission to exclude Jordan from my book. And he made the offer I'd been hoping to hear, to approach the Jordanian authorities and make all necessary arrangements

for me to visit and work in the Hashemite Kingdom. The road to Amman and Petra seemed open, and for the first time I began to think of the ancient trade route that linked Jerusalem to Amman as a route that I might be privileged to traverse, as so many had before me.

About a week before my departure, Ambassador Pickering and I met in his suite at the King David Hotel in Jerusalem. He came with maps and suggestions as to how I should arrange my time in Jordan. He also told me there was a good possibility that I'd be the guest of the Ministry of Tourism, who would provide a car and a driver—just what I needed, since all I had was an international license issued in Israel, and would therefore be unable to rent a car in Jordan. I decided to travel via Cyprus, as connections that way seemed easiest. All my problems seemed to have been resolved.

On arriving in Amman, I had entered two worlds: the Arabic and the diplomatic; Ambassador Pickering's introduction served as an entrée to both. He had told me to call Skip Gnehm at the American Embassy, so I called him from Cyprus. Skip, I had been told, was the number-two man at the embassy. He invited me to be a guest at his home for the duration of my stay in Amman and told me to take a taxi from the airport to the Amra Hotel, where he would meet me. But, when I called, Skip's wife Peggy said he hadn't yet come home, and she came instead to collect me. Richard Murphy, U.S. ambassador-at-large, had decided to pay a surprise visit to Amman, so Skip missed a night at home, and I didn't meet him until the next day.

The next afternoon, I went for a ride with Skip around Amman and the surrounding wadis. Amman is nothing like Cairo. Most of the city is modern, spotlessly clean, with wide avenues. It looked familiar, for all the buildings were faced with the Jerusalem stone that is mandatory in Amman as well as in Jerusalem. The hills looked like the hills of home. There are many more large private homes around the outskirts of Amman than one sees in Jerusalem, but the apartment buildings might have been designed by one of Jerusalem's architects. Perhaps it *was* the same architect. Maybe he moonlights on both sides of the river.

That evening, we attended a reception at the ambassador's home for some new embassy arrivals. It was an opportunity to meet some of the embassy staff as well as many Jordanians, but I had been reluctant to go, fearing that I might be out of place. Nevertheless, I used the evening to make contact with Dr. Hadidi, general director of the Jordanian department of antiquities. Kathleen Boswell, one of the Americans living in Amman, gave me many useful hints and told me what services I ought to request from Dr. Hadidi, who obligingly agreed to give me a letter of introduction to his staff in Petra, which allowed me free entry and the privilege of staying in the old hotel in the center of Wadi Musa, which is now closed to the general public. This advice and the letter of introduction were invaluable. If Kathleen hadn't been prompting me, I would never have known what to ask for.

The next day, Friday, was open, and it seemed like an ideal opportunity to scout out the area around Madaba, the northern end of the Dead Sea, the Jordan Valley, and the areas of Jerash and Ajloun. So we set off at 6:30 Friday morning, heading toward Mount Nebo, from which, according to the Torah, Moses viewed the Promised Land before his death.

What Moses saw was a vision. What I had before me at Mount Nebo was the hot haziness of late summer hovering over the Dead Sea. Of course, I hadn't expected anything else of a visit in early September, and I was prepared to try to work through the haze. It would have been ideal to have postponed the trip until well after the rainy season had begun. But there were two reasons why this couldn't be done: my wife, Anna, was due to give birth, and the book *had* to be finished soon. This view was important, and I was determined to come back several times if necessary. This was,

after all, one of the few viewpoints actually mentioned in the Bible, and it included the northern end of the Dead Sea, the plains around Jericho, the hills of Judea leading up toward Jerusalem, and the Jordan River spilling into the Dead Sea. It would be impossible to see Jericho and the towers of Jerusalem except on the clearest of days, rare even in winter, but I hoped at least to be able to show the outlet of the Jordan into the Dead Sea.

The view from Mount Nebo was without any interesting foreground, so I asked the driver to take me down toward a hot springs called Hamamat Ma'in. The road was likely to have a view similar to the one from Mount Nebo, but at a slightly lower altitude I might be able to include the hills to make the foreground more interesting. This was especially important, since the main subject was very likely to be obscured in haze, and would not be a strong visual element. We found the road, and it was exactly what I'd been hoping for, but by now the sun was high and the haze thick. I marked the spot on my map and decided to return one day late in the afternoon to make the photograph (page 106). Happy to have finally accomplished something after several days in Jordan, we drove to Madaba.

At Madaba, in an Orthodox church, there is a mosaic floor I very much wanted to see. It mapped out the Middle East during the Byzantine period, from the valley of the Nile to the East Bank of the Jordan River, including Sinai, Judea, and Jerusalem—precisely the territory included in this book, so I was curious to see how the Byzantines had pictured the area. The mosaic is fragmentary, with large portions missing, but on it you can clearly see the Nile and a small section of Sinai. Within the map is a diagram of Jerusalem, contained within the walls of the Old City. Jaffa Gate and Damascus Gate are clearly indicated, as is the ancient Roman Cardo, the main avenue running from Damascus Gate toward the Temple Mount. This map was in part what prompted archaeologists to dig under the streets of Jerusalem and excavate the Cardo,

which has now been partly restored and is one of the Old City's major attractions. The map makes up for its lack of precision with an abundance of charm. The most endearing element are the fish swimming down the Jordan toward the Dead Sea, until they actually reach the salty water, where one of them is shown turning around and swimming upstream to avoid being pickled. In fact, this is what tour guides in Israel tell you is grown in the saline waters of the Dead Sea: pickled herring!

Curious to see the northern part of the country, I instructed the driver to drive through the Jordan Valley, along the Israeli-Jordanian border. This area is a mirror image of the Israeli side, the difference being that the Jordan is on your left-hand side as you drive north, instead of on the right. Irrigated by the river, this broad, long valley is dotted with green fields. Even in winter it can be warm here, and in the summer, particularly the late summer, it is often unbearably hot. As we drove past the turnoff for the Allenby Bridge, I could see the hills I know so well on the other side of the valley. Many times I had peered through binoculars at the road I was now traversing. Jordan had then seemed so close and so far away. But now it was Israel that was within view but quite inaccessible. I was reminded of a joke that one of my old roommates, David Thomas, used to tell about the Vermonter, who, asked by a passing tourist for directions, replied, "You can't get there from here."

Leaving the Jordan Valley, we turned roughly east and climbed through the hills to Ajloun, a little town crowned with a small fortress. After a brief visit to the fortress, we followed the winding road through the olive groves on the road to Jerash. The area resembled Samaria on the other bank of the river, though the hills were a little higher and more wooded. We stopped at Jerash, magnificent Roman ruins covering a large area, to which I would have liked to return had I had the opportunity. But there was little time, and I felt I ought to concentrate, for the sake of the book, on the desert. If I'm ever able to return to Jordan,

Jerash will be one of the areas I'll work in. From Jerash, we returned to Amman, where I spent the Sabbath at Skip's home.

During the Sabbath, Skip obtained for me the letter I needed from Dr. Hadidi to enable me to work in Petra and scheduled an appointment for me on Sunday with Mr. Nasri Attalah at the Ministry of Tourism. Sunday morning we went together to Mr. Attalah's office, where I hoped arrangements could be made for a car and driver so that I could begin working that same afternoon. When I presented the letter of introduction from Bob Abrams, president of Abbeville Press, which said that I was working on a book of landscape photographs of Egypt and the Holy Land, Mr. Attalah was taken aback by the book's original subtitle, *Photographs of Egypt, Sinai, and the Holy Land*. Why, he wanted to know, didn't the title include *Jordan*? The truth was that I had asked Abbeville not to mention Israel by name so as not to offend the Jordanians, and I had intended that the term *Holy Land* should include both countries. He felt that Jordan was underrated as a tourist destination and pointed out to me that most people incorrectly associated the phrase *Holy Land* only with Israel and wouldn't realize that the book also included Jordan. He would be happier, he said, if the book's title mentioned all three countries by name. He also said that he'd be glad to assist me by providing a ministry car that very afternoon.

We drove south on the old, winding Kingshighway, a trade route that had served the ancient peoples of the area as a major thoroughfare between Arabia and Damascus. From Amman, this trade route had branched out to the west to Jerusalem and the Mediterranean coast. The Nabateans had effectively exploited their position at Petra, with all its natural advantages, including an abundant supply of water, and controlled the traffic on this road. On the way south, we stopped at Shobak, where I made some photographs of and from the Crusader fortress, perched on a hill overlooking the limestone hills and valleys around it (pages 112–13, 115). As we approached Petra through the little town of Wadi Musa, a change in topography became apparent, the terrain taking on a more rugged appearance. In the distance, the sandstone peak of Jebel Haroun (Mount Aaron) dominated the horizon. The little white mosque on top, where the High Priest Aaron—Moses's brother—is supposedly buried, was to become a landmark for me in the days that followed (pages 126–27).

I got settled in the old defunct hotel in the valley of Wadi Musa just as it was growing dark. As I did so, the two English archaeologists who were sharing it with me introduced themselves. They explained that, while there was a generator, it made so much noise that they preferred the silent illumination of candles, so I made haste to organize my things before it got too dark. I chose a corner room down the corridor from theirs and set up my little camp stove near the table and chair borrowed from other rooms. I was very pleased with this little hotel, known locally as Nazzal's Camp. Nazzal had moved on to bigger and better things since he closed the hotel. He now owned the Holiday Inn in Amman, or so I heard. But Nazzal's Camp suited me perfectly: it was centrally located in Petra itself, with no staff to disturb my loneliness, no bills to pay, and guests whom I would enjoy talking to. Since there were no electric lights in the whole area, I could use one of the vacant rooms at night as a dark-room in which to load sheet film. I lit my candles and cooked my dinner, drinking a little glass of the duty-free whiskey I'd purchased for dessert. Then I went to look for the other two guests, to hear what advice they might offer about Petra. They were quite startled when I opened the door of the dining room where they were sitting together by the light of a candle, for they'd become used to being quite alone in the evenings. I said that it seemed to me like the perfect setting for an *Agatha Christie* mystery, to which they replied that she had anticipated me by setting her *Appointment with Death* in this very hotel. They

suggested that I rise early and hike up to the High Place to get a good view over Wadi Musa. Ambassador Pickering had suggested the same thing, so I set my alarm for five A.M. and went to bed.

The next morning, I took my tripod and camera and set out in the early darkness to find the trail up to the High Place. Using Ambassador Pickering's hand-drawn map as a guide, I found the stairs where the trail begins, just beyond the Roman theater, and started climbing. It took me perhaps half an hour to reach the top, but I had beat the sunrise by at least twenty minutes and began to look around for a good place from which to take my first photograph. I found the view I was looking for on a level spot just above a twisted juniper, looking northwest back toward Nazzal's Camp (pages 120–21). The juniper tree was an unusual find in this part of the world, though I'd seen many on the California coast. Shaked later told me that there was just one spot in Sinai where these trees grow, and this one place in Jordan. Outside of these two places, junipers are not found in this part of the Middle East.

Early though it was, some dust hung in the air, imparting to the scene muted pastels in the red light of dawn. Perhaps because of the antiquities and the ancient culture we know so little about, an aura of mystery hovers over Petra. The soft illumination reinforced this feeling. I wandered about the High Place, nearly stumbling over what had obviously had been a place of sacrifice, where a rectangular trough had been cut into the rock leading to a small spout, through which the blood of the slaughtered animals had flowed. From there I headed down the same way I had come, for on my way up I'd noticed a spot from which I could climb onto the roof of one of the tombs to get a view of the Siq, the narrow canyon through which one enters Wadi Musa. The sun would just be striking the Siq tombs about the same time I came down, and I wanted to make a photograph. My timing was nearly perfect, for the view to the southeast included the tombs and the canyon, but the sun itself was hidden behind the high canyon walls.

The light, as I had hoped, struck the top of the tombs, leaving the canyon itself in shadow. This had all the elements of a dramatic composition that would capture the mystery and awesomeness of the scene. It was almost perfect, and I was pleased (page 119). But as I was folding up my camera, I noticed to my horror that the bellows had numerous tiny holes in its folds, which would admit light and might well spoil the film. I would patch the bellows with opaque black tape as soon as I reached Nazzal's Camp, but for now I decided to push my luck just a little and make another photograph of the tomb facades before going back (pages 122–23). As it turned out, the light leaks *were* numerous, but too small to ruin the film.

After lunch and a little nap at the hotel, I went out that afternoon to see if I could find a Bedouin guide for the next morning to take me to the summit of Jebel Haroun, where Aaron's tomb is supposed to be located. I made arrangements for a Bedouin boy with a donkey to meet me the next morning at 4:30, and then set out on foot for the summit of El-Habis, a hill just beyond Nazzal's Camp topped by the ruins of a Crusader fortress. The fortress itself was of no particular interest to me, but, from it, one has a good view of some of the nearby wadis and their monuments—not the finest Petra has to offer, but there were a lot of them and, from a distance, quite impressive, as much for their facades as for the way they were set in the walls of the sandstone canyons (pages 104–105).

I had few illusions about my Bedouin guide actually showing up by 4:30, when the sky was virtually black. But it was a long walk, and I wanted to reach the summit sometime around sunrise. When I arose, I set off through the blackness to search for the tent where he lived near El-Habis, candle protected against the wind by a lantern I had made from a plastic water bottle (I had forgotten to take a flashlight with me to Jordan). I made it as far as the crest of the hill overlooking the Bedouin's tent, but all was black in that direction, and I could hear no signs

of life. I began to shout for him and was answered only by a rooster and the braying of a donkey, presumably the one that I'd hired. But no human stirred.

By now, my candle was nearly gone. Without it, I could not make out the path, so I shouted a while longer and returned to the hotel. All I could do was wait there. But not for long: in the darkness I could just make out a Bedouin, and I ran after him, thinking he might be looking for me. He was not, but he didn't mind going to get my guide, who showed up with the donkey about 5:15. We loaded the camera and tripod on the donkey and set off for Jebel Haroun, though it was already clear that we wouldn't make the summit by sunrise.

The boy's family had risen by now, and from a little distance their tent was an apparition, glowing deep red, low against the ground. The donkey was unhappy with the early hour and walked at a grudging pace. We tried hitting him a few times to get him moving. Then pulling. I found that pulling him by his rope and walking in front of him could keep the animal moving along at a decent clip. I did this for a few minutes, until I realized that if anyone in our group was an ass, it wasn't the critter with the tail. After all, it was easier to carry the camera than to pull the donkey *and* the camera. But by the time this dawned on me, he had overcome his inertia and kept moving along at a trot when I let go. The boy jumped on, shouting to me to join him, and soon the donkey was carrying me instead of the other way around.

The trail passed Umm-el-Biyara and then turned to the west. Here it looked like a completely different landscape, all shrouded in mist. The summit of Jebel Haroun was hidden in a cloud, so there was no longer any need to reach the summit—from there we would see nothing at all. We went a little further until we had climbed a little ridge, where I decided to stop and photograph the sunrise through the layers of mist. After we'd made tea and had breakfast, we continued, the mist having dissipated, and

reached the summit almost an hour later. Just below the summit was a large covered pool fed by an underground spring from which we filled our canteens.

The little white mosque at the summit had a domed roof from which the Arava—in Israel—could be seen.

We returned from Jebel Haroun the way we had come. After a nap and lunch we reloaded the donkey and began the brief ascent through Wadi Ed-Deir to Ed-Deir ("the monastery"), a giant edifice atop a hill overlooking Wadi Musa. By the time we left, the narrow, winding wadi was entirely shaded, and the walk was as pleasant a walk as might be imagined. Passing some small caverns that most recently had been used by Bedouin families for shelter, we came to the stairs carved out of the rockbed that mark the trail. We followed the stairs to the top, the steps rounded and worn by the feet of countless Nabateans, Bedouin, and assorted tourists. One can only speculate what the purpose of this Nabatean pilgrimage had been and what function this immense facade had served; the place itself gives no clues (page 109). The total height of the facade is forty-five meters, including the urn, which may be seen crowning the landscape as you climb up Wadi Ed-Deir. The sandstone in this area has the texture of melted, dripping chocolate; a nine-meter-high stone urn hovering over this landscape does not even look odd amid all the other odd shapes. (Look closely at the photograph I made of Wadi Musa from the High Place on pages 120–21; you can pick out the silhouette of the urn on the cliffs, almost directly above the building in the center of the photograph.) We climbed over the crest of the hill and saw Ed-Deir directly to our right. It was clear that there was to be had a spectacular view of Ed-Deir's facade and the easternmost cliffs of Wadi Musa, so we climbed the small hill in front of us, and I set up the camera.

Many nineteenth-century landscape photographers deliberately included a person or object of known size in their compositions, in order to give a sense of size and scale. I consider this an artificial device, since there usually are no people about, and I don't see why I ought to make an effort to look for them. The device can also destroy the natural feeling of awe one experiences in the desert, where one rarely knows the size of anything or the distance to anywhere. This ambiguity of scale is an ever-present factor in the desert. Why should I resolve it for the viewer in my photographs? I was nevertheless grateful for two small children playing in the open area near the door to Ed-Deir; without them, you'd never realize just how large this man-made monument is. I made the photograph in the red glow of the setting sun, and we headed down (page 109).

The next day I spent exploring new areas of Petra, but chose the wrong excursions and saw little of interest. I had arranged with the Ministry of Tourism to have a guide pick me up the next morning, Thursday, and take me south to Wadi Rum, a sandstone area that was supposed to be quite beautiful. He showed up in a Toyota Land Cruiser, and we made the two-hour trip south to the government "rest house" in Wadi Rum. The rest house, though new, was obviously not used very often—a bit surprising since the Jordanians seem to regard Wadi Rum as one of their major tourist attractions. Yet there is a complete lack of tourist facilities there, and had I not been blessed with a government Jeep and a guide who knew the area, I would have been able to see nothing at all of Wadi Rum. As it was, I had an excellent guide, Jamal As'Hab, who was as eager to enjoy himself as to show me a good time. After we had had a picnic lunch at the rest house, joined by an English painter visiting the area (a woman named Cherry Pickles), we all set out for a little tour.

Wadi Rum is, of course, only one wadi in a much larger area, but, as the principal wadi, has given its name to the locale. It resembles some of the lovelier sandstone areas of Sinai, and I thoroughly enjoyed myself as we gunned down the sandy wadis at breakneck speed, slowing to maneuver the more difficult parts and to climb. I wanted to find a good area to work in, but I felt that I ought to make a photograph that would look a bit different from what I'd done in the sandstone areas of Sinai. That was a problem: the areas are quite similar. We ended up that afternoon in a lovely canyon, and I made photographs of the canyon walls silhouetted against the evening sky. My photographs from that afternoon were ruined by a strange technical problem that produced colored, wavy lines running through the sky. But since these were the only photographs with which I had difficulties on this trip, I considered myself fortunate. We also had time to explore some more of the wadis and canyons in the dim evening light, and I picked out what I hoped would be a good spot in the morning light.

We left Cherry to herself the next morning and departed early for the spot I'd designated the previous afternoon. But we were quite unable to find it. I grew progressively nervous as the dawn approached, until we finally came to a nice wadi with an open view across reddish dunes to nearby sandstone peaks. I decided to work there at dawn (page 103). After I'd made a number of photographs and felt pleased with the work, we set out in search of a canyon. There, in the canyon of Wadi Abu-Jedaidah, I made a couple photos of the streaming sunlight (pages 124–25), and then we laid out breakfast on a large flat rock from which we could enjoy the view. We had a leisurely breakfast in a beautiful sandstone world. I felt very much at home.

We returned to the rest house to collect our things and then traveled north the way we had come. I was planning to spend the Sabbath at the Petra Forum Hotel, just outside of Petra, and then do some more work on Sunday morning in the vicinity of Petra before heading back to Amman and the north. I had planned that a driver from the Ministry of Tourism should pick me up on Sunday afternoon, but Jamal decided to stay around Petra as well, so that Sunday morning we left together.

Early travelers who came to Petra had to go to quite a lot of trouble to get there, as it was well off the beaten path. This is no longer the case, but I also felt that I had made at least an unusual effort to get there—so I had that much in common with my predecessors. It had been well worth the trouble, and I was sorry to leave. I could have done much more, but it would have seemed irresponsible coming to Jordan and seeing only Petra. The northern part of the country, though not half as spectacular, has its charms as well.

The goal of that Sunday morning, though, was to get a good view of the whole area of Petra, and in that I succeeded. Jamal and I went a few kilometers north along a new road that rose to the crest of a hill commanding a view of Jebel Haroun and the entire sandstone area to the southeast. From this viewpoint it is at least theoretically possible to see the Gulf of Eilat and the mountains of Sinai (pages 126–27). Perhaps the shimmering line near the top of the photograph that I made of Jebel Haroun from Beidha *is* the Gulf of Eilat, and the haze above that Sinai. I would like to believe it, for it would tie together in one photograph most of this book.

There were a couple places I had hoped to photograph as we traveled north, but the haze, which had not been a problem in the valleys and canyons of Petra, defeated me here. So you will see no photographs of the Nahal Arnon, where a miracle was performed for the biblical Jews as they went from Egypt to the Promised Land, nor of the commanding views to be had of the Dead Sea from the east along the Kingshighway.

Save one.

For there was one view I was not going to give up on: the Dead Sea from the hills near Mount Nebo. From here, on a clear day one can see the towers of Jerusalem. Even on a hazy day I hoped to be able to see Jericho, Joshua's first stop in the Promised Land. In the photograph I made that afternoon from the hills above Hamamat Ma'in, the inlet of the Jordan River at the north end of the Dead Sea can be seen (page 106). If the photograph is not exactly what I hoped for, it's attractive nevertheless.

There were still two working days left in Jordan, and I wanted to have a look at the Syrian Desert and the northernmost part of the country. I made arrangements for a driver to meet me early Monday morning at Skip's house to take me to the Syrian Desert to the northeast of Amman—though Ambassador Pickering had warned me that the northern desert is a nearly featureless expanse. There are a few fortresses I hoped might serve as points of interest, and I planned to spend the night at one of them, Qasr el-Azraq. Monday morning we drove east to Qasr el-Azraq, arriving about ten A.M. Any natural beauty this site may once have had was destroyed by the haphazard development of the ramshackle town around it. There was certainly no point in staying overnight, so we returned to Amman. The afternoon, I hoped, might offer a clearer view of Jericho and the Dead Sea. But this was not the case.

There are fine views over the Sea of Galilee and of the Golan Heights from Umm Qais, so this seemed worth trying on my last working day. My guide and driver, Abdul, neglected to tell me until after we'd arrived that photography in this area was forbidden. The morning was lost to photography. We then drove along the Golan Heights from a point just south of the Yarmouk River: from there I might have thrown a stone into Israel.

This had been a whirlwind trip, successful to the extent that I'd accomplished my primary goal and made some good photographs of Petra and the southern sandstone areas. I had covered most of the areas that had traditionally been photographed in the Middle East one hundred years ago, before the area had been carved into warring states. No mean feat; but I can't honestly say that I'd photographed Jordan as it deserves to be. One day, I would like to go back.

Flying over Lebanon and Syria, on the return flight to Cyprus, I felt intense satisfaction. In Sinai, I had felt best walking through an open *farsh*, with the horizon surrounding me. For there

I had been free to explore the outer edges of the horizon in any direction, and to enjoy the panorama that awaited me. In Israel, the horizon line is very often an unreachable destination that lies on the other side of a hostile border. It becomes a reminder of confinement.

During the flight, I read a fascinating article in the Swissair magazine by Dr. Stephan Oetterman about the history of panoramic murals. He wrote:

> *Just as the balloon was a "vehicle without frontiers," the panorama [panoramic painting] was a . . . picture without boundaries. It was the reaction of art to the discovery of the horizon . . . [which] inspired new hopes: there was a promised land just beyond the horizon. . . . The panoramas incorporated a new optical experience: unbounded vision, the total survey.*
>
> *The horizon is not a boundary of which modern man is painfully aware. It has become a mere metaphor since it can be crossed at supersonic speed and is perforated by the rays of millions of television sets. The experience of the horizon as a form of limitation today lies behind us. Yet for the traveller in Goethe's day it was, once one had become aware of it, an optical constant from which there was no escape. The wanderer might well quicken his pace or even take the mail coach—the horizon still surrounded him like a prison, accompanying him wherever he went as doggedly as his own shadow.*

Looking down at the glittering Mediterranean coastline off Syria and the mountains of Lebanon to the south, it seemed to me that even if I hadn't achieved complete freedom, at least I'd had the illusion of it—for a while. The landscape on the eastern side of the Jordan River was no longer a puzzle, but something acquired through experience: I had crossed forbidden boundaries, and I had been to the other side of the horizon.

PAGE 103: *View to the north from Wadi Burdah, in the area of Wadi Rum.*

PAGES 104–105: *Tombs in the Siyagh, from El-Habis.* "The fortress [of El-Habis] was of no particular interest to me, but, from it, one has a good view of some of the nearby wadis and their monuments—not the finest Petra has to offer, but there were a lot of them and, from a distance, quite impressive, as much for their facades as for the way they were set in the walls of the sandstone canyons."

PAGE 106: *North end of the Dead Sea, from Hamamat Ma'in.* ". . . there was one view I was not going to give up on: the Dead Sea from the hills near Mount Nebo. From here, on a clear day one can see the towers of Jerusalem. Even on a hazy day I hoped to be able to see Jericho, Joshua's first stop in the Promised Land. In the photograph I made that afternoon from the hills above Hamamat Ma'in, the inlet of the Jordan River at the north end of the Dead Sea can be seen. If the photograph is not exactly what I hoped for, it's attractive nevertheless."

PAGE 109: *Jebel Ed-Deir and Wadi Musa.* "One can only speculate what the purpose of this Nabatean pilgrimage had been and what function this immense facade had served; the place itself gives no clues. . . . The total height of the facade is forty-five meters, including the urn, which may be seen crowning the landscape as you climb up Wadi Ed-Deir. . . . We climbed over the crest of the hill, and saw Ed-Deir directly to our right. It was clear that there was to be had a spectacular view of Ed-Deir's facade and the easternmost cliffs of Wadi Musa, so we climbed the small hill in front of us and I set up the camera. . . . I made the photograph in the red glow of the setting sun, and we headed down."

PAGES 112–13: *View from Shobak Castle.* The layering and folding of the rock are impressive features.

PAGE 115: *Shobak Castle.* A Crusader castle on the Kingshighway between the southern end of the Dead Sea and Petra.

PAGE 119: *Canyon of the Siq.* ". . . on my way up [to the High Place] I'd noticed a spot from which I could climb onto the roof of one of the tombs to get a view of the Siq, the narrow canyon through which one enters Wadi Musa. The sun would just be striking the tombs about the same time I came down, and I wanted to make a photograph. My timing was nearly perfect, for the view to the southeast included the tombs and the canyon, but the sun itself was hidden behind the high canyon walls."

PAGES 120–21: *Wadi Musa from the High Place.* I made this photograph "on a level spot just above a twisted juniper, looking northwest back toward Nazzal's Camp. . . . Early though it was, some dust hung in the air, imparting to the scene muted pastels in the red light of dawn. Perhaps because of the antiquities and the ancient culture that we know so little about, an aura of mystery hovers over Petra. The soft illumination reinforced this feeling."

PAGES 122–23: *Tombs, upper Siq.* After I photographed the Canyon of the Siq, I climbed down and made this frontal view of the facades of those same tombs when the light had completely illuminated them.

PAGES 124–25: *Canyon of Wadi Abu-Jedaidah.* "There, in the canyon of Wadi Abu-Jedaidah, I made a couple photos of the streaming sunlight, and then we laid out breakfast on a large flat rock from which we could enjoy the view. We had a leisurely breakfast in a beautiful sandstone world. I felt very much at home."

PAGES 126–27: *Jebel Haroun from the northeast.* "The goal of that Sunday morning . . . was to get a good view of the whole area of Petra, and in that I succeeded. Jamal and I went a few kilometers north along a new road that rose to the crest of a hill commanding a view of Jebel Haroun and the entire sandstone area to the southeast. From this viewpoint it is at least theoretically possible to see the Gulf of Eilat and the mountains of Sinai. Perhaps the shimmering line near the top of the photograph that I made of Jebel Haroun from Beidha *is* the Gulf of Eilat, and the haze above that Sinai. I would like to believe it, for it would tie together in one photograph most of this book."

Israel

Countless times we drove from Jerusalem to Sinai, first heading east on the descent to the northern shore of the Dead Sea, then turning south and driving along the western shore until we had passed Har (Mount) Sodom, a mountain of salt. The Dead Sea Works is just below Har Sodom, and at this point, the Dead Sea looks more like a series of shallow industrial pools than a natural body of water. But who could call it water? Devoid of life, it's more properly sludge. The Dead Sea Works, with its thick covering of white dust, blends in with the landscape completely. South on the pot-holed, poorly graded road is a winding descent as you leave the hills of the Judean desert and head through the Jordan Rift Valley, whizzing through the blinding white glare of the Arava and Negev deserts. Somewhere along this fairly straight stretch of road, we usually get out of the Jeep, stretch, and make our first cup of coffee, perhaps under the shade of an acacia tree, which recalls Sinai.

The landscape around the tree, however, is nothing like Sinai. Here is almost no sandstone or granite, but chalk and limestone. The land is often flat, except for soft, rolling hills with an occasional chalky cliff. The landscape is much more restrained than Sinai, not given to the wild extremes of high mountains and rocky crags, nor to the fantastic shapes of sandstone.

It is also a much more *restraining* landscape than Sinai, for it is a far cry from virgin wilderness. Settlements and even small cities abound, around which are systems of roads, factories, and neat patches of irrigated green fields growing an amazing variety of crops under difficult conditions. Desert towns in Israel are, for the most part, neat, pleasant places, even the largest of them such as Beersheba, in the Negev, and Arad, in the Judean desert. But this is not wilderness. Even the unpopulated districts are used, though just how is not always visible at first glance. Many desert areas serve as firing and training ranges for the Israel Defense Forces.

And so we come to the other restraining influence, the border with Jordan. Almost anywhere you go in the Judean desert, you see the mountains of Jordan winking at you, their peaks catching the light. This is a rift zone, the locus of a geological upheaval that lifted the granite, sandstone, limestone, and chalk layers in Jordan high above the level on our side. The softer rock weathered away, leaving occasional splashes of varicolored sandstone, such as those around Petra. The rift zone begins in the north, and in its path you find Lake Kinneret (the Sea of Galilee), the Jordan River, the Dead Sea, and, finally, the Gulf of Eilat and the Red Sea. The valley forms a natural barrier between Israel and its eastern neighbor. This landscape, which, naturally, I would wish to explore from both sides, is open only on one, and that only to a point. As you draw close to the border, you begin to find things like mine fields and electronic fences, which not only prevent drawing closer, but prohibit photography in their general direction. The electronic fences are now being extended farther south, along the northern shore of the Dead Sea, and it will soon be impossible to go near the water, except at approved tourist spots that charge admission. If you want to take a photograph of this area, you'd better go quickly! On our side of the border there are military zones even in the "wilderness" areas. When they're not being used for target practice, I'm free to enter: but just try to find out exactly when they are and are not in use. The only time they're certainly not used is on the Sabbath, when, as an observant Jew, I can't use them either. Despite the difficulties, Judea is beautiful enough to merit the effort of working in it. Caught between the anvil and the hammer, I do my best.

There was no need to grapple with all these problems as long as Sinai was available. I knew that my camera and I weren't going to be welcome guests there forever, so *Sinai first!* was my motto. Though we had promised ourselves for a long time an exploratory trip to the Judean desert, it wasn't until after Sinai had been returned to Egypt that Shaked and I actually embarked.

Previously, all I had seen of the Judean desert was from the road along the Dead Sea. From the road, you look down on the sea and, to the west, up at the cliffs that run along the sea's entire length. Here and there are spots of interest to tourists, such as the mud baths and hot sulfur springs. And if such things don't interest you (they don't interest me), then there are Masada and Ain-Gedi. Masada is truly fascinating, but the reader has learned by now that my love of landscape excludes the kind of place to which tourists come by air-conditioned busloads. For me, Masada has lost its natural charm. For the tourist who has never experienced the desert, a trip to Masada *might* be counted a desert experience.

Ain-Gedi has a certain advantage over Masada: to see anything, you must walk. Not far, but even to hear the waterfalls you're going to have to exert yourself. My father will testify to this. He has a bad leg, and it was a warm day when we took my parents there. Just twenty meters beyond the toll gate (it's a nature reserve for which you must pay admission), he asked, "Are you taking me to die in the desert?" This ancient Jewish cry had much the same effect on me as it had on Moses. Unlike Moses, however, I was under no divine injunction to continue, so we turned back.

One day I shall be sufficiently motivated to photograph the lovely falls and pools of Ain-Gedi and will be able to bring myself to work under the stares and questions of visitors. That day has not yet come. I like my deserts deserted. Even in grade school, my teachers told me that I lacked social skills.

The most beautiful area of all in the Judean desert lies on the cliffs running from the north of Ain-Gedi to the south above Har Sodom (pages 148–49). Here are magnificent views toward the east, particularly in the late afternoon when the reddish light drills through the thin haze that hovers over the Dead Sea on even the clearest days.

The view from the entire length of these cliffs is always much the same. Always the Dead Sea and the mountains of Jordan above. Yet the view never grows monotonous, for the Dead Sea is a spectacle of changing, almost iridescent colors, polychromatic displays caused by many factors, foremost the color of sunlight as it filters down over the hills to the west. This can be anything from a dull yellow on hazy days to a vivid red during the last moments of a clear day. After sunset, the light grows blue and then deep purple, often retaining a touch of red on the higher mountains in the distance, a phenomenon known as alpenglow. Another factor is the level of salinity in the water, which varies from area to area. Finally, there is the depth of the water, anything from one-half meter in some of the salt evaporation pools to several hundred meters in the deepest parts.

Anna and I used to dedicate every Thursday during our first couple of years in Israel to exploring the Negev and Judean deserts. On one of these trips, we stood below Arad looking down on the rounded hills of the Judean desert and the Dead Sea, hills cast in a pale pink, the surface of the water a multitude of quiet pastels. It was then that I first felt the need to photograph the desert and to do so in color.

The cliffs that tower over the Dead Sea are three to four hundred meters above sea level. But the Dead Sea is not anywhere close to sea level—it is "dead" because, at nearly four hundred meters (1,312 feet) *below* sea level, it has no outlet, and all the minerals deposited in it remain after the water that brought them in evaporates. So the drop from the cliffs to the sea is seven to eight hundred meters (2,297 to 2,625 feet). Over the centuries, water has cut canyons that are one of the most distinguishing characteristics of the Judean desert. Above them I have often roamed in my Jeep.

My first trip to this area was with Shaked and one of his friends. We spent five days wandering through narrow, rocky wadis. The foray was meant to be more of a get-to-know-you

excursion than a working trip. It seemed to me that the intimacy I had established with Sinai would have to be earned here in the same way, by spending a lot of time exploring and working. But as we emerged from the wadis, and I saw these magnificent canyons and the view they commanded, I began work in earnest. The light was clear, and visibility to the east was superb. It was a good thing I managed to make some photographs then (pages 148–49), because in the intervening years we've been suffering from warm winters and a shortage of rain. Without water to keep the air free of dust and without the cold to hold down evaporation from the Dead Sea, a thick haze builds up that makes it almost impossible to photograph. So it has been unrelentingly hazy during recent years, and the days when I've sat on the edges of the canyons staring glumly far outnumber the days of good visibility.

Standing on the hills overlooking the Dead Sea, you also have a view to the west. These views are not as large, not as dramatic, but they are in a way the essence of the Judean desert's charm. Here and there among these relatively low, rounded hills you see a herd of camels or a Bedouin shepherding his flock. From a little distance it may be difficult to tell the sheep from the low scrub on which they feed (pages 158–59). Climbing at sunrise to the peak of one of the small mountains, Har Itai, Har Namer, Har Harduf, you are treated to the view of a sea of hills aglow with the reddish yellow light of dawn. Here you can be alone as in few other places in the Judean desert (pages 130–31). To the east, the Dead Sea is nearly always visible through gaps in the hills. Just north of Nahal (Hebrew for *wadi*) Tse'elim, this area is pleasant and untouched.

Except for a thin strip just above the cliffs and canyons, the areas to the north are almost completely taken up by Israel Defense Forces live firing ranges. Even on a day when they're not shooting, you risk burial under a cloud of fine white dust raised by a passing column of tanks. In the area adjacent to the firing zones, the sound of

exploding shells or a passing jet fighter occasionally prompts eagles to take wing, and then you can watch them soaring high above the canyons.

To the south lies the desolation of Har Sodom, a mountain of salt continuously growing, only to be reduced by weathering. Its summit consists of rounded domes of salt, its cliffs of jagged salt sculptures. Hardly anything lives around this mountain. Even climbing on the salt domes is treacherous; many consist only of a thin crust over a hollow interior. Virtually every evening affords a spectacle of changing hues associated with the salt flats and evaporation pools (pages 146–47, 155). Just as the sky begins to turn blue, the lights of the Dead Sea Works come on and are echoed by its Jordanian neighbor across the water. This is an eerie place; that you are seeing nothing more than industrial evaporation pools does not diminish its strange beauty. Climbing down the western side of Har Sodom, you come to a spot as desolate as any I have ever seen. Here is a flat plain of soft, crusty salt through which a wadi called Nahal Pratzim has cut its way. On a map, it looks like the web of veins in a leaf. When you stand on the plain above this wadi, it looks smooth enough, but as you draw closer you notice the tissue of veins etched into the salt. Here and there, in the depth of this crusty-looking wadi, an acacia grows: for below the surface are streams of water. Enclosed in a world of white powder, the delicate acacias are a lovely sight, a victory of life in a world of lifelessness (pages 156–57).

The Judean desert rises in steps from the Dead Sea up to Jerusalem, which stands nearly eight hundred meters (2,625 feet) above sea level. There is the climb from the Dead Sea up the canyons to the level above, which includes the area from Bikat Horkaniya in the north to the territory below Arad in the south. Desolate though it may be, this part of the desert has never been entirely unpopulated. At Horkaniya, for example, there are remains of an ancient Maccabean fortress and a Byzantine church. The Byzantine monks were not the first ascetics to make their home in the Judean desert. The Essenes, a sect that lived in and around the caves near Qumran, preceded them. Scattered throughout the Judean desert are ruins of fortresses that have passed through many hands. A fortress on a hill in Bikat Horkaniya, though no longer used, is still part of a live firing area of the Israel Defense Forces. Other fortresses, such as those protecting the entrance to Wadi Kelt above the plain of Jericho, are still in place and have been supplemented with newer structures.

From Qumran to Horkaniya completes the first step, and from Horkaniya (at 248 meters/814 feet) to Har Muntar (at 515 meters/1,690 feet) is the second. This is a grand view, which I've long wanted to photograph, but I've never had the good fortune to be there on a day with sufficient visibility. Looking east from Har Muntar there is, of course, the Dead Sea, and almost the entire Judean desert is visible from north to south. To the northeast are the Jordan Valley and plains near Jericho. To the southwest is Herod's fortress at Herodian, and almost due west are the hills on the edge of Jerusalem, the tower of the Hebrew University on Mount Scopus, and the tower on the Mount of Olives. From Har Muntar to the Mount of Olives is just eight kilometers (4¾ miles), and from Har Muntar to the Dead Sea is another twelve (7½ miles). The width of this small desert is just twenty kilometers (12½ miles). It would fit into Sinai's back pocket.

Descending from Har Muntar to the south, you reach Nahal Kidron (the Kidron Brook of the Bible), the spring that flows from Silwan at the southeast corner of the Old City of Jerusalem all the way to the Dead Sea. It is rotten with sewage, white with detergent, and thoroughly disgusting (pages 166–67). Nothing, I suppose, could pollute the Dead Sea, but this stream of sewage fouls everything else in its path. Following this downstream just a little way, the wadi narrows, becoming a steep canyon. There, descending the cliff on the western side, is a walled compound with gigantic buttresses enclosing the Orthodox monastery of Mar Saba. Spectacular for its setting in the midst of a desert canyon, this is where I made one of my favorite photographs in the Judean desert (page 161). Ironically, I had to wait for a particularly hazy day—though not too long—to diffuse the light of the rising sun in order that the soft curves of the canyon and hills above show to their best advantage, without heavy black shadows.

Following Nahal Kidron toward its source, you don't go more than a few kilometers before coming to the first patches of cultivated land and a small village. Already you are in the ring of villages and settlements that surround Jerusalem. Along the crest of the Judean Hills, which descend from Jerusalem in the north to Hebron in the south, you find trees and green fields within view of the desert. The Judean desert is desert because of these hills, which prevent the rain from reaching it. The Judean desert is therefore a high desert, a desert surrounded by mountains that trap the rain clouds.

Continuing to climb in Nahal Kidron, you arrive at the southeast corner of the Old City of Jerusalem. Above you are the massive walls that guard the extreme southern edge of the Temple Mount. From here you can see the dome of the Al-Aqsa Mosque. Within a few hundred meters lies the very spot where Abraham prepared to sacrifice his son Isaac, and the site of the First and Second Temples. The ruined Temple has now been supplanted by the Dome of the Rock, also known as the Mosque of Omar (pages 170–71). This perfectly proportioned gold dome sparkles and enlightens the city from the earliest moments of daylight, even before the sun's first rays strike from above the desert hills. The tiled blue structure from which the golden dome rises rests on a base of white stone that blends in with the paving stones of the Temple Mount. Blue and gold appear to float, a cloud hanging in the sky.

Most people, residents and tourists alike, see Jerusalem during the hours of bright daylight.

Since virtually every building is made of the highly reflective white-to-rose-colored Jerusalem stone, the city during the day is a glittering mass of white. Without sunglasses you are forced to look down at the ground. There is so much light that it does the opposite of what we expect it to do, blinds rather than illuminates. The time, then, to see the city is at twilight and first light. In the early morning, the eastern sky slowly fills with a deep red light, at first just a thin line of red above the horizon. Slowly it expands upward in an arc that becomes more of a golden orange as it takes the sky. The sun is not yet up, so the walls of the Old City to the west are still dark patches, but already the gold and silver domes begin to glow. When the sun's rim finally ascends above the crest of the Mount of Olives, it illuminates the higher buildings with a brilliant red glow. Here is Josephus's description of the Second Temple in the light of dawn: "The exterior of the sanctuary did not lack anything that could amaze either mind or eye. Overlaid on all sides with massive pieces of gold, it reflected in the first rays of the sun so fierce a flash that those looking at it were forced to look away as from the very rays of the sun. To strangers as they approached it, it seemed in the distance like a mountain clad with snow; for any part not covered with gold was of the purest white." The Dome of the Rock now echoes the brilliance of the ancient Temple.

Then the light begins to play on the Temple Mount itself, illuminating first the arched stone gates at the western side. The line of light moves quickly east, until it reaches the top of the city wall. From there, it descends down the wall, illuminating the Golden Gate and the valley below. For a few moments the whole city is ablaze with dawn, but, as the sun rises, its color changes to white, and the aura that enveloped the city dissi-

pates, becoming a bright, white glare (pages 174–75).

DeClerq, Salzmann, Bonfils, and Frith made lovely studies of these scenes. Their finest prints have both a delicacy and a depth for which modern black-and-white photographic papers are no match. They were careful and passionate workers who spared no effort to make the finest possible photographs. No detail was too small for them to explore, but they never neglected the larger views that put everything into perspective. For all this, they were never able to capture the most evocative mood of all in Jerusalem, that of the early morning and late evening. Their films were simply not sensitive enough, and they could not record color. Especially in Jerusalem, I feel very strongly that I've continued their work, taking it in a direction they would have been glad to go themselves.

The holiness that infuses the city is most palpable in the soft light of the moon and in the hours that are neither day nor night. It was in the earliest moments of dawn that the priests in the Temple would begin preparing the Temple service, and during the day's last seconds that they would conclude it. Those are even now the hours during which men, wrapped in their prayer shawls, may be seen hurrying toward the Western Wall to offer their prayers in place of the Temple service. I am often among them, and at these times I like best to walk along the top of the ramparts on the eastern wall of the city, looking toward the Mount of Olives and sensing the spare presence of the desert just beyond the hills.

Here, close by the Temple Mount at dawn, the light washes over you, casting a brilliant aura on everything. For a moment, the light seems to burn everything it touches, but when that moment of brilliance passes, you are still standing, unconsumed and at peace with the world.

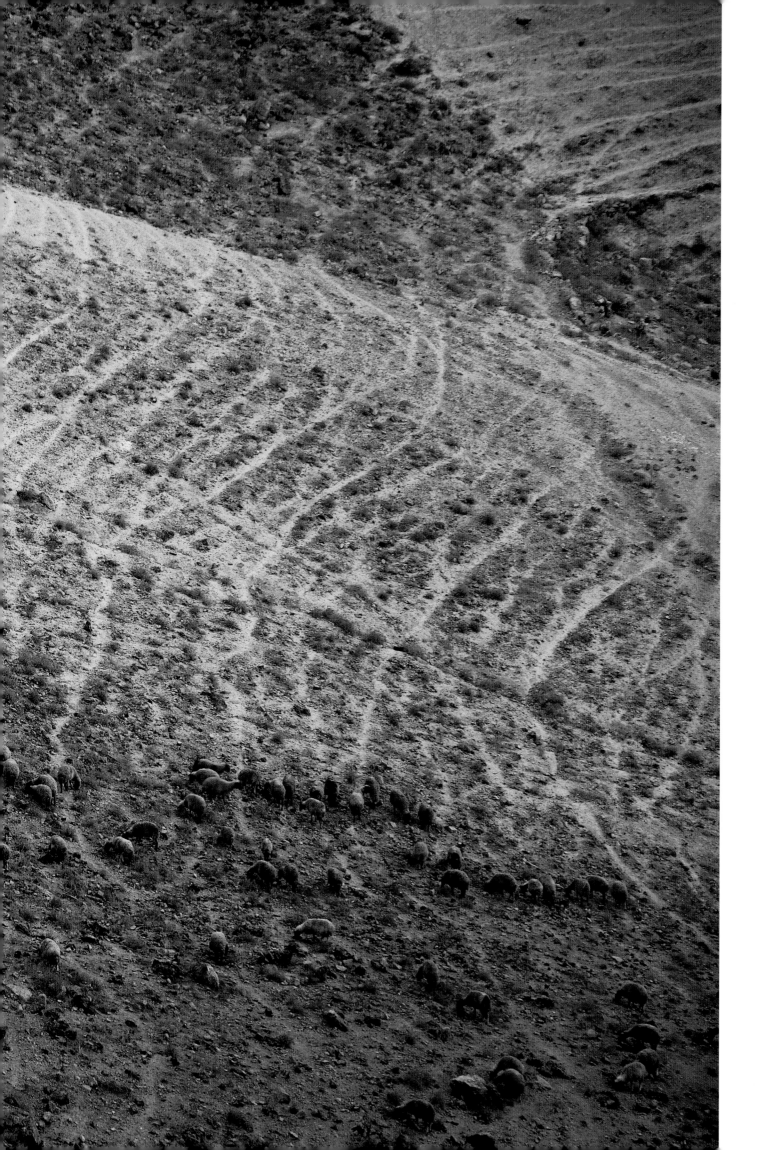

PAGE 129: *Poppies and almond blossoms, Judean hills.* The flowering blossoms and wildflowers of early spring enliven the dry, rocky hillsides of Judea. The hills around Jerusalem are loveliest in spring.

PAGES 130–31: *Har Haduf and Har Itai from Har Namer.* "Standing on the hills overlooking the Dead Sea, you also have a view to the west. These views are not as large, not as dramatic, but they are in a way the essence of the Judean desert's charm . . . . Climbing at sunrise to the peak of one of the small mountains, Har Itai, Har Namer, Har Haduf, you are treated to a view of a sea of hills aglow with the reddish yellow light of dawn. Here you can be alone as in few other places in the Judean desert."

PAGE 132: *Christian Quarter in snow, Old City.*

PAGE 135: *Dome of the Rock and Al-Aqsa mosques.*

PAGE 139: *Train, Nahal Refaim.* The train tracks from Jerusalem to Tel Aviv pass through some of the most beautiful parts of the Judean Hills. Unfortunately, the route was of no use to commuters, and the little train hardly runs anymore.

PAGES 140–41: *Wadi Kelt with storm clouds.*

PAGES 142–43: *Monastery of St. George, Wadi Kelt.* After massive rains, Wadi Kelt was flowing with volumes of rainwater—in addition to the regular flow from the spring of Ain-Kelt, the source of the wadi. From its source, the wadi flows past the monastery to the Plains of Jericho.

PAGE 144: *Ain Kelt.* This is the source of the water in Wadi Kelt.

PAGE 145: *Village of Carmel.* These small homes with the domed roofs date back to the period when the village was Jewish. Some still bear signs of Jewish ownership, such as decorative Stars of David or an indentation on the doorpost for a *mezuza.* A new Jewish settlement, established after the 1967 war, overlooks this Arab village.

PAGES 146–47: *Southern end of Dead Sea.* "Virtually every evening affords a spectacle of changing hues associated with the salt flats and evaporation pools. Just as the sky begins to turn blue, the lights of the Dead Sea Works come on and are echoed by its Jordanian neighbor across the water. This is an eerie place; that you are seeing nothing more than industrial evaporation pools does not diminish its strange beauty." The pipe that runs through the center of the photograph is used to pump out mud.

PAGES 148–49: *Dead Sea from Mitzpeh Matmon.* "The most beautiful area of all in the Judean desert lies on the cliffs running from the north of Ain-Gedi to the south above Har Sodom. Here are magnificent views toward the east, particularly in the late afternoon."

PAGE 150: *Road below Har Sodom, Dead Sea* (top); *Salt flats, Dead Sea* (bottom).

PAGE 151: *Evaporation pools from Har Sodom.*

PAGE 152: *Feeder Canal, Dead Sea.* One of the canals used to transfer water between pools.

PAGE 153: *View south from Jebel Harmun.*

PAGE 154: *Har Sodom and the Dead Sea from Har Namer.*

PAGE 155: *South end of the Dead Sea, with storm clouds* (top); *Salt flats at dusk, Dead Sea* (center); *The Dead Sea from Har Namer* (bottom).

PAGES 156–57: *Acacias in Nahal Pratzim.* "Climbing down the western side of Har Sodom, you come to a spot as desolate as any I have ever seen. Here is a basically flat plain of soft, crusty salt through which a wadi called Nahal Pratzim has cut its way. On a map, it looks like the web of veins in a leaf. When you stand on the plain above this wadi, it looks smooth enough, but as you draw closer you notice the tissue of veins etched into the salt. Here and there, in the depth of this crusty-looking wadi, an acacia grows: for below the surface are streams of water. Enclosed in a world of white powder, the delicate acacias are a lovely sight, a victory of life in a world of lifelessness."

PAGES 158–59: *Sheep grazing, Judean Desert.* "Here and there among these relatively low, rounded hills you see a herd of camels or a Bedouin shepherding his flock. From a little distance it may be difficult to tell the sheep from the low scrub on which they feed."

PAGE 160: *View from Har Hetzron to east.* In the foreground are the low hills of the Judean Desert; in the background, the higher mountains of Jordan rise above the Dead Sea.

PAGE 161: *Monastery of Mar Saba, Nahal Kidron.* Ironically, I had to wait for a particularly hazy day to make this photograph, in order to soften the light and prevent harsh black shadows from obscuring the wadi below.

PAGES 162–63: *Hills above Ain-Fawarra.*

PAGES 164–65: *Oasis of Ain-Farat.* This oasis is located just a short distance from the Jerusalem suburb of Neve Ya'akov, but I doubt if more than a few of its inhabitants are aware of the existence of a desert oasis at their very doorstep.

PAGES 166–67: *Nahal Kidron.*

PAGES 168–69: *Jerusalem from the Alon Road.* As you drive from the area of Jericho up to Jerusalem, the towers on the Mount of Olives come into view. Just the other side of the Mount of Olives is the walled city.

PAGES 170–171: *Old City from Mount Scopus.* Here a large section of the wall that encompasses the Old City is seen. The sunlit wall faces east; the gate in the center of that wall is known in Hebrew as the Mercy Gate, in English as the Golden Gate. The gold dome is the Mosque of Omar, also called the Dome of the Rock. The silver dome is the Al-Aqsa, which was damaged some years ago and since this photograph was made has been replaced with a new, unsilvered dome, more like that of a century ago.

PAGES 172–73: *Damascus Gate.* This is the largest gate on the north wall of the Old City. During the Second Temple period this gate was within the outer walls, which extended much farther north.

PAGES 174–75: *Temple Mount and Old City from east.* "The sun is not yet up, so the walls of the Old City to the west are still dark patches, but already the gold and silver domes begin to glow. When the sun's rim finally ascends above the crest of the Mount of Olives, it illuminates the higher buildings with a brilliant red glow. . . . Then the light begins to play on the Temple Mount itself, illuminating first the arched stone gates at the western side. The line of light moves quickly east, until it reaches the top of the city wall. From there, it descends down the wall, illuminating the Golden Gate and the valley below. For a few moments the whole city is ablaze with dawn, but as the sun rises its color changes to white, and the aura that enveloped the city dissipates, becoming a bright, white glare."

PAGE 176: *Temple Mount from north end.* I made this photograph from the roof of the Al-Amariya School, adjacent to the northern end of the Temple Mount. The hill covered with graves on the left is the Mount of Olives, a Jewish cemetery. The little cupola in the foreground is a Crusader structure that may be concealing a site of unexcavated Second Temple artifacts.

PAGE 177: *Western Wall and Temple Mount.* Taken from a building in the Jewish Quarter, this view shows the Western Wall ("Wailing Wall") below the Temple Mount. Beyond the Dome of the Rock is the tower and campus of the Hebrew University of Jerusalem.

PAGES 178–79: *Old City at dusk.* Almost every photographer of the 1850s made a similar view showing this road (delineated in this photo by the lights of passing cars), with the city walls above. The color of the evening sky is entirely natural, and the city walls glow with the brilliance of the warm light that they reflect from the sky.

PAGE 180: *Mamilla Street.* This street is just outside the Jaffa Gate of the Old City, and is slated for urban renewal. The architecture, though nothing grand, is an echo of the Al-Nasser Mosque, Cairo.

PAGE 181: *Courtyard, Meah Shearim.* I couldn't resist including this view from outside the walls of the Old City, though this was one of the first areas to be built outside the walled part of the city.

PAGES 182–83: *Southern wall of Old City and Temple Mount.* The new building in the upper left is a *yeshiva*—rabbinical seminary—in the Jewish Quarter. In the shadow of the palm-tree is the Dung Gate, the gate closest to the Western Wall and the Temple Mount. The Romans used to dump their refuse here to show their scorn for the Jews. (We are still here, but where are the Romans?)

PAGES 184–85: *The Western Wall, Birkat HaHama.* Once every twenty-eight years, the planets and sun are in the same alignment as they were at the time of Creation. At sunrise on this day, one may make the blessing: "Blessed are Thou, O Lord our God, King of the Universe, who does the work of Creation." This blessing, called Birkat HaHama, is the event for which these people have gathered.

PAGES 186–87: *Golden Gate from the Mount of Olives.* The Golden Gate, known in Hebrew as the Mercy Gate, is the one through which the Messiah will enter the city. It is spotlighted here by a burst of light that managed to break through the low morning storm clouds, as I was waiting to make the photograph. After that brief break in the light, there wasn't a touch of sunlight all day. There are patches of snow below the city wall. The Jewish graves in the foreground are part of the large cemetery on the Mount of Olives.

PAGE 188: *Old City from eastern ramparts.* I rose before sunrise to make this photograph from the top of the eastern wall near the Lions Gate. The Temple Mount rises almost to the height of the city wall. Frith made a similar view some one hundred years ago, but in his view the city walls were not visible, and he was unable to impart to the scene the golden light of dawn. The cranes to the right of the Dome of the Rock are in the Jewish Quarter, and the church to the right of these is on Mount Zion. The church tower in the upper right-hand corner is the Lutheran Church of the Redeemer, whose tower offers a pleasant view from the center of the Old City.

PAGE 189: *Moon setting over the Jewish Quarter of the Old City.* Although it was still well before sunrise, there was enough light in the sky from the east to make this photograph of the city with the moon setting in the west.

PAGE 190: *The Valley of the Cross and the Israel Museum.* An urban landscape in the new part of the city.

Neil Folberg
in a Desert Land

Neil Folberg at work along the Dead Sea coast

The word for photographer in nineteenth-century Hebrew was *tsayar shemesh*, "painter of the sun." The Arabic expression *mussawwra shamsi* still has the same meaning. Neil Folberg has breathed new life into this old concept, that the sun does the painting. Looking at his brilliant landscapes, we imagine him sitting behind his camera, waiting for the sun to rise and color the sky purple, cast shadows upon the mountains, and make the sand dunes translucent. Then all Folberg has to do is release the shutter, capture the scene created by the sun, and transmit it to us.

Sun, desert, exotic landscapes, and holy places have drawn photographers to the East since the earliest days of the camera. Now Folberg comes, with a vernacular completely his own, to record the desert and the two ancient civilizations that perch on its borders, on the shores of the Nile, and on the mountains of Jerusalem. Like the photographers of old, Folberg takes us—armchair travelers—on a journey to distant lands.

THE EARLY PHOTOGRAPHERS

The history of photography in the Near East begins a mere two months after the invention of the medium was made public at a joint session of the Academies of Sciences and Fine Arts in Paris, on August 19, 1839. The French government purchased and published "free to the world" the details of the photographic process. Within days, opticians' shops were crowded with buyers seeking to obtain a "daguerreotype apparatus," as the camera was then called. One Parisian optician, N.M.P. Lerebours, declared that famous sites could now be recorded with precision rather than interpreted by the artist's imagination, and he dispatched photographers all over the world to capture "remarkable views." He sent painters Horace Vernet and Frédéric Goupil-Fesquet to Egypt and the Holy Land where, before the end of 1839, they visited ancient temples along the Nile and the cities of Jerusalem, Nazareth, and Acre. Their images appear in *Excursions Daguerriénnes: Vues et monuments les plus remarquables du globe* (1840–44).

The word *photography* comes from the Greek *photos*, meaning light, and *graphein*, to draw. A photograph is a fixed permanent image produced upon a surface through the interaction of chemicals and light. The ancestor of the process is the *camera obscura*, or "dark room" in Latin, first described in the tenth century by an Arab scholar, Ibn al-Haitham al-Hazin. It consisted of a small room into which light was admitted through a tiny hole, throwing an inverted image of whatever was outside onto the opposite wall. The technique was used to view eclipses of the sun and as an aid to drawing. Yet the images created by the light were not permanent.

Three men are credited with ushering in the age of photography: Joseph Nicéphore Niépce (1765–1833), Louis Jacques Mandé Daguerre (1787–1851), and William Henry Fox Talbot (1800–1877). It was Niépce who, in 1826, took the first extant photograph, from the window of his study near Chalon-sur-Saône in France, by exposing to light for about eight hours a pewter plate coated with layers of bitumen of Judea, a substance similar to asphalt. He considered the image his first successful effort at "reproducing nature." He then went into partnership with Daguerre, who had worked with a *camera obscura* to create stage sets for the Diorama Theater. But Niépce died before they perfected the invention, which, as a consequence, was named after Daguerre.

The daguerreotype process used a wooden camera and, as "film," copper plates polished with silver. A plate was inserted into the camera, exposed to light for about fifteen minutes, then developed in a chemical bath. The image on the plate was a positive, which could be seen only by one person at a time, holding the plate at a certain angle. Moreover, there was no way to make multiple "prints" from the unique positive. Daguerre and Niépce's son unsuccessfully tried to market the new product, announcing it as "a chemical and physical process which gives Nature the ability to reproduce herself." But only after the French government purchased the process and divulged it to the public did the ideas capture the popular imagination.

Meanwhile, working almost simultaneously across the Channel, Talbot independently developed a method of recording images on paper negatives. An English scientist, linguist, and mathematician, Talbot began to experiment by treating paper with solutions of salt and silver nitrate. He then exposed the paper to light in a camera, creating a reverse image—a negative—from which many positives could be printed. The process was called calotype or Talbotype. Although Talbot's images lacked the sharpness of the daguerreotypes, his negative-positive technique made it possible to print and publish images in quantity, and it became the preferred photographic method.

Both the daguerreotype and the calotype were soon succeeded by the wet-collodion process, published by Frederick Scott Archer in 1851 and destined to dominate the market for the next thirty years. Archer employed glass plates as negatives, which he sensitized to light by coating them with collodion, a mixture of ether, alcohol, and nitrocellulose. The collodion-coated glass plate was dipped into silver nitrate solution, inserted wet into the camera, and exposed to light. The plate had to be processed immediately, which meant that, when a photographer was working away from the studio, he had to travel with a darkroom—either a tent or a wagon.

Some of the very first photographs taken outside of France came from Egypt and the Holy Land, thanks to Lerebour's *Excursions Daguerriénnes*. Even before this, there is evidence of photography's affinity for the East. Shortly after Daguerre secretly demonstrated his invention to François Dominique Arago, director of the Paris Observatory and the noted scientist who persuaded the French government to purchase the process, Arago declared: "To copy the millions and millions of hieroglyphics which cover the great monuments of Thebes, Memphis, Karnak . . . one would need legions of draftsmen and

twenty years. With a daguerreotype, one single man could do this huge task."

The painters who were sent to the Orient by Lerebours—Horace Vernet, known for his biblical scenes, and Frédéric Goupil-Fesquet, art teacher and author of textbooks on drawing—were joined by Vernet's nephew, Charles Marie Bouton, who, with Daguerre, was proprietor of the Diorama Theater that had led Daguerre to his photographic experimentations. The three traveled with the daguerreotype equipment and with Daguerre's manual, *Histoire et description du procédé nommé le Dagueréotype*, a seventy-nine-page illustrated booklet, written in cumbersome scientific style, which, nevertheless, did not diminish its popularity; the volume appeared in thirty editions and was translated into eight languages within a year of publication.

Vernet, like other painters after him, began to use photographs in addition to sketches to provide himself with material for future paintings. "We know how often the *pencil* is proved to be treacherous and deceptive, while on the other hand the *fac simile* of the scene must be given by the aid of the *photograph*," wrote the Reverend Albert Augustus Isaacs in his 1857 book *The Dead Sea*. Ironically, the supposedly objective camera could be almost as subjective as the pencil or the brush, since the men behind the lens also "edited" their views. Most photographers chose to depict only famous sites, which they showed in the most dramatic manner. Throughout the nineteenth century it is an exotic and romantic Orient that is captured by the camera, as well as holy places and other locations selected for biblical association.

General interest in the Orient, as the Near East and North Africa were called in the nineteenth century, was rekindled by Napoleon's invasion of Egypt on July 1, 1798. Throughout the early 1800s, explorers and dealers, agents of European governments and private collectors, Egyptians, and others began to plunder temples and tombs, and treasures were shipped to Europe at an ever-increasing rate.

Fascination with the ancient civilizations of Egypt and Mesopotamia and the recognition of the strategic value of the countries that form the land bridge connecting Europe, Asia, and Africa were intermingled with one other element: reaction to the industrial and scientific revolutions, begun with the Enlightenment in the 1730s. Rather than relying on reason and empirical facts to combat ignorance, superstition, and church dogma, by the late eighteenth century, a romantic reaction set in and brought about changes in art and literature. In Germany, *Naturphilosophie* grew under the influence of Goethe, and in England Romantic poets rebelled against dry logic and science. There was also a religious awakening as men sought to return to a simple belief in God, to a faith that had been shaken by recent scientific discoveries. The Bible was reexamined in the light of new theories of creation, and theologians debated the role of formulated knowledge versus the tenets of Christianity. The age of American exploration of the ancient Near East began in 1838 — a year before photography was born — when theologian Edward Robinson went to the Holy Land, Bible in hand, and tried to identify sites mentioned in the Scriptures, reaffirming their authenticity through their contemporary place names, whose origins went back to ancient Hebrew roots. Robinson's results appeared in *Biblical Researches in Palestine, Mount Sinai, and Arabia*, published simultaneously in England, Germany, and the United States in 1841.

Curiosity about the Orient, political awareness of the military and commercial importance of the area, and a renewed zeal for identifying the origins of the Bible brought east an ever-increasing number of visitors. As Victor Hugo wrote in 1829, in his introduction to *Les Orientals*, "The whole Continent is leaning eastward." Archaeologists, biblical scholars, pilgrims, missionaries, merchants, diplomats, soldiers, adventurers, royalty, reporters, authors, poets, painters — and photographers — arrived by boat and disembarked at Alexandria, Jaffa, Beirut, or Constantinople. Steam had replaced the power of wind and sail on the high seas, and crossing the Mediterranean had become less dangerous. Thus ordinary tourists also came — products, too, of the Industrial Revolution, which had created a new leisure class with the means and the time to travel. The nineteenth-century tourists became the photographers' best customers, since they sought to buy souvenirs of their sojourns in the Orient. Listed in Murray's *Handbooks* of the 1840s and in Baedeker's *Guides* soon thereafter were the shops in every major city where photographs could be purchased.

Pen, brush, and, later, the lens recorded and transmitted the impressions of travelers in ancient lands and foreign civilizations. It was a world full of paradoxes. "The Orient . . . escapes convention," noted French painter and writer Eugène Fromentin in his 1858 book *Une Année dans le Sahel*. "It lies outside all disciplines, it transports, it inverts everything, it overturns the harmonies with which landscape painting has for centuries functioned." The Orient fascinated, puzzled, and, at times, repelled; but it left no one indifferent, as is evidenced by the hundreds of books that came off presses in Europe and the United States, bearing such titles as *Those Holy Fields* or *In the Footsteps of the Man of Galilee*.

Not all the literati were favorably impressed. William Makepeace Thackeray found Jerusalem "unspeakably ghastly," and Herman Melville called her "a barbarous city." The most scathing remarks came from the pen of Mark Twain, who recorded his impressions from an 1867 visit in *The Innocents Abroad:* "Renowned Jerusalem itself, the stateliest name in history, has lost all its ancient grandeur, and has become a pauper village; the riches of Solomon are no longer there to compel the admiration of Oriental queens." Twain was disappointed, as were many others, when the Orient, and especially the Holy Land, did not meet with his expectations. But "Jerusalem!" wrote Pierre Loti in 1895, "What dying splendour clings about the Name. How it radiates still, out of the depths of time and dust! Almost I feel that I am guilty of profanation in daring place it thus, at the head of this record of my unbelieving pilgrimages. . . . Jerusalem, recognizable from all other towns . . . gloomy and high, enclosed within its battlements, under a dark sky."

The impact of the Orient on Western painters was always more simply positive, perhaps because they were sensuously enchanted by the brilliant colors and challenged by the bright sunlight. Less cerebral than their literary counterparts, they allowed themselves to be lured by the sights. There were magnificent remains of ancient civilizations, Roman ruins in Baalbek and Palmyra, temples and pyramids by the Nile, Crusader forts on the banks of the Jordan. There were exotic bazaars, with sun-drenched fruits and fragrant spices, whirling dervishes, dancing girls, and mysterious harems. Artists like Tissot and Holman Hunt were no longer satisfied with religious imagery inspired by Renaissance art. They came to the Holy Land, which had changed little since biblical times, in search of landscapes and people. They found flocks and shepherds in the hills of Judea, olive trees at Gethsemane, and in the desert, nomads and camel caravans.

Among the painters who became known as the "Orientalists" were representatives of every major stream of nineteenth-century art, from Romanticism to Realism to Impressionism. Maryanne Stevens discusses the encounter between Western art and the Islamic world in her introduction to the catalogue for a recent exhibition, *The Orientalists: Delacroix to Matisse.* "The repercussions of such visits [to the Orient] can be seen in their effects on two broad areas of artistic concern, subject matter and technique." And, she adds, "in the case of Delacroix, Fromentin, Renoir and Matisse the influence of the Orient was on their technical development as painters, especially in their handling of light and color."

The crystal-clear, harsh sunlight of the Orient was highly prized by early photographers, when insensitive emulsions meant that exposure times were long and when still landscapes were subjects preferred to people, whose movement made them mere blurs. It is interesting to note that both painters and photographers depicted identical sites from similar vantage points, since, like all other foreigners, they followed prescribed routes. Travel in that part of the world was difficult and dangerous, especially in Palestine, where, until the end of the nineteenth century, there were hardly any hotels or paved roads. Travelers slept in tents and had to hire guides and horses to take them from place to place. The guides, known as dragomans—*turgemans*, or translators—also served as bodyguards and suppliers of tall tales. Unfounded traditions, often passed on by ignorant priests, produced such mythical sites as "Jacob's Well" or "Joseph's Pit." From a welter of photographic clichés we can conclude that every person with a camera was directed to the exact same spots, on top of the Mount of Olives or in front of the Giza pyramids.

Several hundred photographers traversed the Orient before the end of the nineteenth century, amateurs and professionals, adventurers and explorers. Even though art for art's sake was not their goal, some produced very fine images and are worthy of note.

As we have seen, the first men who were sent to photograph Egypt and the Holy Land, Vernet and Goupil-Fesquet, were both painters. Next to photograph the Orient was Maxime Du Camp, a writer who learned photography when he was sent by the French Ministry of Education to conduct a survey of the Orient. From 1849 to 1851 he traveled with another Frenchman, the novelist Gustave Flaubert, who was on a similar mission on behalf of the Ministry of Commerce and Agriculture. Of the 214 calotypes Du Camp took, 125 were published in *Égypte, Nubie, Palestine et Syrie,* the first travel book illustrated with photographs. Its publication was also the first use of mass-produced prints, issued by the firm of Louis Désiré Blanquart-Edvard.

Flaubert appreciated his companion's work. He himself was moved to give out "a loud cry" when he first saw the Sphinx, and he claimed that "no drawing that I have seen conveys the proper idea of it—best is an excellent photograph that Max has taken." Flaubert found that the journey broadened his previous concepts: "the Orient extends far beyond the narrow idea I had of it. . . . Facts have taken the place of supposition." The facts were not always pleasant. In Jerusalem, "old religions quietly rot. One steps in dung, with ruins around . . . everywhere . . . a very sorry sight," he wrote in *Voyage en Orient*.

The first use of the camera as a scientific instrument in the study of archaeology occurred in Jerusalem, in 1854, when another painter-turned-photographer, Auguste Salzmann, arrived to help prove Louis-Félicien Caignart de Saulcy's theories about the age of ancient monuments and architecture in the city. De Saulcy had explored a tomb that he attributed to the Judean kings. He also identified other remains as dating back to the time of Solomon, rather than to the Greek and Roman periods, as was commonly believed. When he declared that Sodom and Gomorrah might yet be found, the French archaeological establishment and the popular press were enraged. He was accused of never having been to the Holy Land and of forging the drawings in his book *Voyage autour de la Mer Mort*. Salzmann, the "prototype of the intelligent photographer whose work should inevitably make the historical sciences progress significantly," according to de Saulcy, was going to provide photographic evidence to support his dates.

Salzmann's 174 large calotypes appeared in Paris in 1856, under the title *Jérusalem, Études et reproductions photographiques des monuments de la Sainte Ville*. The publisher was Blanquart-Edvard, who used albumen paper, a paper he coated with egg whites, to print the positives. This improved process resulted in prints that were clear and brilliant, qualities that have survived to this day. The now rare portfolio was an artistic triumph but a commercial failure.

Salzmann is unique among the photographers of the often-depicted city of Jerusalem, per-haps because he spent several months there and got to know her well. As a painter, he may have been especially sensitive to texture and form, and he used his camera almost like a brush. A detail captured at close range became an abstract, a surrealistic composition. He employed the harsh sunlight to create a tension between the city's white stones and dark shadows. Salzmann did not think of himself as a photographer, but as a painter and archaeologist. Yet today he is remembered for his photographs. This is especially noteworthy since the survey of Jerusalem was his only venture in photography.

The possibilities for the commercial exploitation of the camera were obvious both to publishers and photographers from the start. One of the first men who combined these two professions was Francis Frith. Born in England in 1822, he was raised as a Quaker and knew the Bible well. In 1850 he established a printing company and learned how to photograph. Eventually he founded F. Frith & Co., in its day the largest printing and publishing firm in the world. He was marketing books, albums, and stereoscopic photographs—pairs of photos that, seen through a special viewer, create three-dimensional images. He published postcards by the thousands, as well as such special editions as the *Queen's Bible*, illustrated with photographs of great artistic quality.

Frith traveled all over the Near East between 1856 and 1859. He visited Syria, the Holy Land, and Sinai, and ventured some fifteen hundred miles up the Nile. In order to take various kinds of photographs , he carried with him three different cameras, one for stereoscopic views, one standard-size camera, and one large, 16 x 20 camera. (Since negatives were contact printed, a large-format camera was necessary.) He carried his cumbersome equipment, complete with glass plates and the chemicals required in the wet-collodion process, in a wagon that also served as darkroom and sleeping quarters. To ward off curious natives, he declared that it was his harem, "full of moon-faced beauties, my wives all!—and great was the respect and consideration which this view of the case procured for me." Typical of the early photographers in the area, he had to deal with temperatures that at times climbed to 130 degrees Fahrenheit (54 degrees Celsius): "Now, in a smothering little tent, with my collodion fizzing—boiling up all over the glass the instant that it touched . . . it is truly marvelous that the results should be presentable at all." Frith soon published some of his "results" in *Egypt and Palestine, Sinai and Palestine, The Holy Bible,* and other volumes.

The first major photographic survey of the Orient under British auspices began in Jerusalem in 1864. Church and state in England demanded maps of the Holy Land then, as Darwinism was casting doubts on the truth of the Bible and as world events like the Crimean War were demonstrating the fragility of the strategically critical Ottoman Empire. Maps were needed to verify biblical sites and to secure military intelligence. Captain Charles W. Wilson, of the Royal Engineers, arrived in Jerusalem in June 1864, supposedly to help find additional sources of water for the overcrowded city. With his team came Sergeant James McDonald, who became an excellent photographer. The team received permission to survey and photograph the area of the Dome of the Rock, which was normally closed to non-Moslems. Maps, plans, and eighty-five photographs were published in the 1865 *Ordnance Survey of Jerusalem,* which emphasized topography and general architecture rather than holy places and monuments.

Also in 1865, the Palestine Exploration Fund, still active today, was founded in England. Under its auspices, Wilson went to survey Lebanon and returned to Palestine several times with other photographers, H. Phillips, H. H. Kitchener, and Gottlieb Schumacher. In 1868–69 he led an exploration to Sinai, with photographer James McDonald, hoping to help "trace the route taken by the Israelites in their wandering through the wilderness." The three-volume *Ordnance Survey of the Peninsula of Sinai* conveys the power of the desert as captured through McDonald's lens.

In 1867, French photographer Félix Bonfils and his family settled in Beirut, where they founded the *Maison Orientale.* Félix had been to Lebanon in 1860 with the French expeditionary force, sent to protect Christian Maronites in their battle with the Druze, and he liked the country. For five decades he—and, later, his wife and son—produced some of the finest images in and of the Near East.

A mere four years after his arrival in Beirut, Bonfils reported to the Société Française de Photographie that he had prints of Egypt, Palestine, Syria, and Greece—some 15,000 prints and 9,000 stereoscopic views—made from 591 negatives: "My proofs are principally pictures of Jerusalem and various panoramas." Heat, added Bonfils, "has presented the greatest difficulty to overcome," since it made his wet-collodion boil. By 1871 he managed to secure outlets for his photographs in half a dozen major cities. He also began to photograph the people of the Orient, listed in his catalogues under "*costume divers.*" It was a departure from the landscapes and city views most commercial photographers produced, perhaps because Bonfils lived in the area and knew the inhabitants.

The *Maison* left behind a comprehensive body of work, the result of a commitment to the Orient that visiting photographers lacked. Aware that modernization was about to change the face of the land, the resident photographers set out to capture the present. "Progress, the great Trifler, will have swiftly brought about the destruction of what time itself has respected. . . . Before that happens, we have tried, so to speak, to fix and immobilize it in a series of photographic views," wrote Adrien Bonfils, who continued the work of the *Maison* after his father's death in 1885.

Frank Mason Good was a British photographer who visited the area at the same time that Félix Bonfils settled there. An accomplished technician with a special feeling for the countryside, he recorded natural landscapes rather than monuments and holy places.

Most of the early photographers in the Orient were Christians, born and trained in Europe. The first indigenous photographers were Armenians, Christians native to the area who, unlike most Jews and Arabs, had no religious scruples against creating "graven images." Local inhabitants also had an ingrained suspicion of modern and foreign inventions, most succinctly expressed by Mohammed Ali, the Viceroy of Egypt, when he saw his first daguerreotype in 1839: "It is the work of the Devil!" Abdullah Frères were two Armenians who had converted to Islam and served as the court photographers to Sultan Abdul Hamid II (1876–1909). Eager to show the West the reforms he was launching, his photographers were dispatched to document progress and change. In 1893, fifty-one large folios of these photographs were presented to the Library of Congress in Washington, D.C., a fine record of life in the Ottoman Empire at the end of the nineteenth century.

At about the same time, in Jerusalem, the American Colony began to sell the photographs of others and then to take photographs of its own. Founded in 1881, the colony produced magic lantern slides and stereoscopic photographs that were used in the West as aids to schools. In 1896 G. Eric Matson joined the colony. He taught himself how to photograph and, for some fifty years, traveled and recorded events and daily life all over the Middle East. In 1946 he left the war-torn area and came to the United States, where he died in 1977. Some 20,000 of his negatives are now in the Library of Congress.

As the nineteenth century was drawing to a close, technological advances were simplifying the process of photography. Coated with a gelatin that contained silver salts, the dry plate replaced the wet-collodion method; it could be bought ready-made and developed long after exposure. Travelers no longer needed to drag wagons or tents along to use as darkrooms. As the speed of film increased, exposure times became shorter, and the camera was freed from the tripod and could be carried by hand. At Thebes, in 1890, George Eastman took a photograph with his Kodak No. 1 and ushered in the era of photography by the masses. When tourists began to produce their own souvenirs, commercial photographers in the Orient faded from the scene.

PHOTOGRAPHY AS ART: FROM EMERSON TO FOLBERG

Neil Folberg is a twentieth-century artist who brings with him some of the qualities that were the trademarks of the early photographers of the Orient. Born and trained in the West, he committed himself, like Félix Bonfils, to live and work in the East. He has a great sensitivity to the land, to remote places not yet known, a sensitivity that reminds us of Frank Mason Good. He approaches his subjects with a mystical feeling, reminiscent of Auguste Saltzmann.

There is also a direct intellectual link between Folberg and the early European and American practitioners, who saw photography as an art form and who set new rules for using the camera faithfully, beginning with Peter Henry Emerson in England, a century ago. A physician and amateur photographer, he lectured on photography as a pictorial art. Later he published the substance of his lectures in *Naturalistic Photography for Students of the Art*, explaining that photography had the potential to become a great creative art in its own right and that it did not have to follow the formulas of painting. He searched for a new scientific basis for pictorial photography.

It was Emerson who, in 1887, awarded a prize, in a competition sponsored by a periodical called *The Amateur Photographer*, to a young American, Alfred Stieglitz. A great believer in the artistic possibilities of the camera, Stieglitz worked to obtain for the medium recognition as an art. A fine technician, he advised photographers to choose their subject carefully, study the lines and the lighting of the scene, then wait for the moment when everything was in perfect balance—adding that he waited for three hours during a fierce snowstorm in 1893 for his famous *Fifth Avenue, Winter* photograph.

Among the young photographers Stieglitz encouraged was Paul Strand, who became known for photographing in sharp detail close-ups of plant life and driftwood. His powerful landscapes conveyed a strong sense of place. Strand expected the person behind the camera to have integrity, to be direct and sensitive without resorting to tricks or manipulation. His approach became known as "straight photography."

Strand's work influenced Ansel Adams to give up the piano and devote himself to photography. A lover of the wilderness, Adams became well known for his representation of rugged mountain terrain. He adopted Strand's straight photography approach and went on to develop a system that gives the photographer control over the final results by mastering the interrelation of brightness, exposure, and development. By measuring the light level of different sections of the scene and correlating the results with exposure and development procedures, the photographer can foresee the printed image in his mind. Explains Beaumont Newhall in *The History of Photography:* "Guesswork is eliminated, and the photographer can concentrate upon the esthetic problems, secure in the knowledge that his results will not only be of technical excellence, but will embody his subjective interpretation of the scene."

In 1932, reacting against pictorial photography that had become too restrictive, Adams, with Edward Weston and other photographers, founded "Group f. 64," its name reflecting the practice of setting lenses at the smaller apertures to achieve maximum depth of field and thereby capture nature's variety of light and texture at its sharpest and richest. At age sixteen, in 1966, Neil Folberg first attended Ansel Adams's Spring Workshop in Yosemite. Over the years he main-

tained his connection with Adams and, like him, developed a special feeling for the wilderness, hiking in the High Sierra, in the Rondane Mountains of Norway, and in Yugoslav Macedonia. It was in the open spaces of Sinai, in 1979, that Folberg began to use color, and he has been photographing desert landscapes ever since.

The desert has been a mystical place since ancient times. Sinners and saints hid there, rebels and prophets. The Israelites wandered in the desert for forty years, and it was there that God gave them the law. Folberg shows us the limitless expanse of the desert, the light effects upon the vast emptiness, the fine jagged mountain ridges that rise to the sky. At the edges of the wilderness he documents the interplay between desolate vistas and cultivated areas, where there is water, where palms grow in oases, where the Nile rises to paint a lush green ribbon.

Folberg's keen eye detects nature's geometry: reeds and their shadows, windswept dunes, rolling hills in the Judean wilderness. With equal facility, he records the brutal force of creation in the craggy slopes of Mount Sinai, and the softness of a Japanese-like landscape, when summer haze envelops a distant valley. Folberg startles us with his versions of well-known views when he presents them in a different light, from an unusual angle, avoiding photographic clichés.

Folberg's mastery of technique and the fresh authenticity of his vision assure him a place in the history of photography. In addition, there is the magic of his colors: there are canyons in pale gray limestone, grainy pink granite, and onyx in many shades; the Dead Sea turns from chrome white to soft blue; the walls of a desert cave flow and glisten like melting ice. The sun and the moon lend him a hand, tinting the dunes, casting a new light upon Jerusalem for Folberg to record. A century and a half ago, Louis Jacques Mandé Daguerre first described photography as "a chemical and physical process which gives Nature the ability to reproduce herself." It is in the spirit of these words that Neil Folberg works.

Acknowledgments

Many people have assisted in some way in the making of these photographs; I am indebted to all of them. My wife, Anna, not only endured the numerous absences from home, but served as my best and most objective critic. Her good humor and common sense guide me in all that I do. My parents have been the other source of encouragement: nothing could have been accomplished without them. The passing of my father, may his memory be blessed, has left a gap in my life which will never be filled, but my mother's constant energy and good cheer fill my life with light.

As I look back on this work, I remain grateful to all those who assisted me so many years ago. First, my guides: Mordi Farkash (who is now an engineer) and Shaked, who is still a close friend and very active in promoting conservation of natural resources at the Society for the Protection of Nature in Israel.

The U.S. diplomats who were so very helpful have moved onto other posts. Ambassador Thomas Pickering, who arranged the trip to Jordan, later became the U.S. Ambassador to the United Nations where I was able to visit him on occasion; Ambassador Skip Gnehm afterwards served as ambassador to Kuwait and until recently at the U.N. Skip has just received a wonderful position as head of the U.S. Foreign Service in Washington, D.C. where I hope to see him now and again if he doesn't manage to visit me here in Jerusalem. Despite the peace treaty with Jordan, I have had no further contact with the Jordanian Ministry of Tourism and the Department of Antiquities who were so helpful in Jordan. I am glad to say that an Israeli no longer needs diplomatic contacts to visit and work in Jordan.

All the editors and production staff with whom I worked at Abbeville have moved on, but the editor for this new edition, Meredith Wolf Schizer, has been a delight; we have enjoyed many "working" lunches together! Mark Magowan and Bob Abrams have, of course, remained at Abbeville. Over the years they have continued to seek the right opportunity to get this book back into print, for which I am very grateful. Bob has always been particularly friendly and helpful, and I hope we'll find other projects to work on together.

All of this work was privately funded, mostly by a dedicated group of collectors who supported it through the purchase of prints, and the enthusiasm with which they viewed it. There are far too many to list all of them, but to all of them I am deeply grateful. Foremost among them, Rod Holt has not only been a supporter, but a close friend who has seen our family through difficult times.

Here I must thank the many "Visionaires," the staff of Vision Gallery and Vision Framing, who through the years have become close friends of our family and contributed to the success of this book and these photographs. Vision Gallery's days in San Francisco have finally come to an end, to the sorrow of scores of photographers throughout the world. Though the new Vision Gallery in Jerusalem can never hope to replace the scope of my father's original Vision, it is my hope that some of us will find a common home there.

Index